The Thirteenth Doctor

The Doctor Who Episodes of Jodie Whittaker

Jonathan Ward

Contents

Preface

Not so long ago I was watching the Doctor Who Christmas special The Church on Ruby Road - the first full episode by Russell T Davies with Ncuti Gatwa. Despite my high expectations (which were a consequence of glowing advance media reviews of this episode and also the fact that I quite enjoyed the Davies penned anniversary specials with David Tennant), I found The Church on Ruby Road, with its surfeit of talky EastEnders style domestic scenes and near complete lack of plot, a rather tedious and empty experience.

An interesting thought struck me during the episode. Chris Chibnall would have been absolutely pilloried for The Church on Ruby Road had he written it! And yet Russell T Davies got away with it! That seems to be the fate of Chris Chibnall though when it comes to Doctor Who. He literally couldn't do anything right in the eyes of some fans. Chris Chibnall's Doctor Who era is regarded by many (though obviously not all) to have been a complete disaster. But is this fair?

Chris Chibnall's version of Doctor who definitely what you might call a mixed affair. Series eleven seemed to be an attempt to make the show simpler and the Doctor more friendly. It had an obvious desire to be topical and educational. None of these elements worked in my opinion. The show was boring, the 'nice' Doctor was bland, and the social commentary was patronising and self-satisfied. Although it may sound an awful lot like one at times during the section on series eleven, this book is not intended to be a sustained one-sided rant against Chris Chibnall's Doctor Who. Like many Doctor Who fans, I was dismayed at how bad series eleven was when it finally hit the screen. This was the worst the show had been since it returned in 2005 and my frustration is evident. Later in the book I will have some nicer things to say Chibnall's Who.

Series eleven was an unbelievably bland, tedious and

underwhelming season of Doctor Who. This was easily the worst series of the show since it returned in 2005. You could argue that it might be the worst season of the show ever made. Sure, Classic Who had wobbly sets and rubbish special effects but it at least had interesting sci-fi ideas most of the time. It had things happening and the Doctor was always (or nearly always) a fascinating character. Series eleven of Doctor Who had no interesting ideas, a Doctor that was so uninteresting you wouldn't have missed her if she wasn't even there, and a strange air of indifference on the part of the showrunner.

Series eleven was supposed to be a bold new reboot for the show to draw in new viewers and give established fans the fresh coat of paint they had been seeking. And yet, there was a tired feel to series eleven. Chibnall's Doctor Who in series eleven felt like something on its last legs and bereft of ideas rather than the opening salvo of a brave new dawn. Chibnall brought absolutely nothing to this beloved show in series eleven. Where were all the ideas we assumed he had stored up? What was Chibnall's great masterplan?

Far from energise the show, series eleven left many fans less enthused than ever. Could you blame them? In Britain, 10.6 million people watched The Woman Who Fell to Earth. By the time of the tedious finale The Battle of Ranskoor Av Kolos, the viewing figures were 6.6 million. This trend would get worse in series twelve. The series twelve finale The Timeless Children drew only 4.6 million viewers - the worst figures since the show came back in 2005. The shows placed around Doctor Who season twelve on the BBC's Sunday night schedule, like Country File and Call the Midwife, actually beat Doctor Who in the ratings. Embarrassingly, it was even speculated that Doctor Who's dismal viewing figures were artificially inflated by impatient Call the Midwife fans tuning in at the end to see if Doctor Who had ended yet!

Yes, there are mitigating circumstances - like the advent of YouTube, streaming, catch-up, and people simply not watching traditional 'live' television in the same way that they used to. Technology is rapidly changing the way that we consume television or entertain ourselves. However, series twelve was broadcast in the winter during a number of wild storms in Britain when there wasn't much else to do but batten down the hatches, stay inside, and watch television. One would think this would be the ideal circumstances for high viewing figures. This wasn't like a Capaldi season thrown to the wolves in summer (when people go out a lot more) and up against big live sporting events.

The argument that no one watches television anymore because they have YouTube and streaming services doesn't completely wash. Everyone still owns a TV. If you put something really good on television that attracts positive word of mouth and becomes an 'event' then people will watch it. The slide in viewing figures for Doctor Who began in the Capaldi era so it's not a new phenomenon. Chibnall had the chance to make Doctor Who event television again but blew it by producing a terrible season with series eleven. You can't blame anyone who bailed out of series eleven. If it wasn't called Doctor Who I wouldn't have lasted four episodes.

It's hard not to think that a lot of the damage for this slide in ratings was done in series eleven. Viewers were understandably curious to see the first female Doctor at the start of series eleven but once this curiosity had been sated they found a show hardly worthy of their time (especially in an era when there are so many new sci-fi and fantasy shows jostling for our attention). Series eleven made a mildly interesting if patchy start but then sank without trace after the abysmal one-two punch of Arachnids in the UK and The Tsuranga Conundrum (surely two of the worst episodes of Doctor Who ever made).

While series eleven never quite got this bad again it wasn't much good either. Episodes like Demons of the Punjab, Kerblam!, and The Witchfinders were just bland and forgettable. They never really grabbed your attention or contained anything that would make you want to return. By the time of the tedious finale The Battle of Ranskoor Av Kolos, no one really cared anymore. Chris Chiball had somehow squandered all the goodwill and curiosity that greeted the arrival of series eleven. Hopes and expectations were so high when The Woman Who Fell To Earth neared its premiere and it was deflating and depressing indeed that series eleven proved to be so tepid and disappointing.

Series twelve was more of a fan service series. Series twelve is desperately trying to making Doctor Who a big deal again by throwing huge surprises and twists at the audience. And it works - almost. It almost works. If series eleven was a 1/5 season, then series twelve is a 3/5 season. And yet, with a couple more good episodes in the vein of Spyfall, series twelve could easily have been a 4/5 season. The Spyfall episodes were terrific and after the astoundingly bad Orphan 55 the season managed to get back on track with the twists and surprises of Fugitive of the Judoon.

We then had to endure the disappointing Praxeus and Can You Hear Me? before The Haunting of Villa Diodati and Ascension of the Cybermen managed to steady the ship again. And then, frustratingly, we had The Timeless Children - a finale that never really managed to deliver. Frustrating would be an apt description for season twelve in that it could have been a surprisingly excellent season if Orphan 55 had been replaced with a better episode and The Timeless Children had been really good. In this scenario, the mediocre Praxeus and Can You Hear Me? would have have been easier to tolerate as filler episodes before the third act of the season arc kicked in. The controversy of the Timeless Child arc is probably something that will be forgotten in time. Plenty of crazy things have happened in Doctor Who before and will do again.

While I am always surprised to learn there are people who enjoyed series eleven (it's perfectly fine if people enjoyed that season but it was so dull I'm just amazed that anyone derived much enjoyment out of it), I am not surprised by any and all reactions to series twelve. I can understand people who think it was great, I can understand people who hated it because of the Timeless Child arc, and I can understand people who are in the middle and thought it was merely average. At the very least Chris Chibnall provoked reactions with series twelve. There was - at last - stuff to talk about and debate. It was a sign that Chibnall was moving in the right direction.

Although Chris Chibnall asserts that he avoids reading anything about his version of Doctor Who, series twelve definitely feels like a reaction to series eleven. It almost feels like Chibnall studied the most salient criticisms of series eleven and made some changes. Series twelve is better than series eleven. There are a couple of two-parters, the return of the 'cold open', returning villains, returning characters (as we'll see in Fugitive of the Judoon), and an arc. You even get a big two part finale. Of the ten episodes in series twelve, four are good, two are passable enough, and four are duds. That's patchy but still a considerable improvement over series eleven where - The Woman Who Fell to Earth aside - all of the episodes were either boring or atrocious.

The best thing about series twelve is that stuff happens. It sounds obvious and stupid I know but it's true. Stuff HAPPENS. In series eleven nothing happened. There is more stuff to react to in Spyfall or Fugitive of the Judoon than the whole of series eleven put together. The return of an arc is welcome too. You might not like where Chibnall ultimately goes with this arc but at least there is one. We have a reason to keep watching. The writing got a mild shake-up too with Nina Metivier, Maxine Alderton and Charlene James all becoming contributors. Maxine Alderton in particular was a welcome addition.

Even the TARDIS interior (which was hideous in series eleven) looks better in series twelve. The vast checklist of things in series eleven that we complained about (like the lack of an arc, no high stakes, dull stand-alone episodes, no returning villains or characters) has been noted. An effort has been made to make the show better and more compelling with bigger stakes and a sense of danger for the characters. There are plenty of big guest stars like Stephen and Fry and Goran Višnjić and a couple of surprise ones too. Series twelve is not a home run but you can see that everyone tried to raise their game and make it better. There is a lot of effort on show - especially in the two-part Spyfall openers. These episodes feel more like a big finale than a premiere and that's exactly what Chris Chibnall's Who needed. We appreciate the effort. Series twelve is inconsistent but it is much better than season eleven.

After the so-so Revolution of the Daleks, the pandemic and budget constraints cast serious doubt on the future of Doctor Who. To the credit of Chris Chibnall though he decided to go for broke and came up with the six episode season called Flux. Now, the Flux arc was patchy and didn't have a very good ending but most of it was at least entertaining and in War of the Sontarans and (especially) Village of the Angels we got two of the best episodes of the Chibnall era. Chris Chibnall, contrary to series eleven critics like myself, WAS capable of making decent episodes of Doctor Who. He'd already proved that in series twelve with excellent episodes like Spyfall Part 1 and The Haunting of Villa Diodati.

The problem is though that Chris Chibnall could never seem to find any consistency during his time as showrunner. There was always a clunker just around the corner. This was perfectly illustrated by the 2022 specials which ended his tenure. Eve of the Daleks was quite good (if not tremendously exciting) and The Power of the Doctor was terrific.

Sandwiched between these two specials though we had Legend of the Sea Devils - which was atrocious. This all makes the Chris Chibnall frustrating in that we know he was capable of a better show than he actually delivered most of the time.

Despite all the brickbats thrown at Chris Chibnall during his time on Doctor Who I suspect that, in time, his era might be remembered slightly more fondly than it was received. When you factor in that Chibnall didn't have much money to juggle either you can cut him more slack than he was afforded during his run on the show. At the very least he did keep the show going and end on a high note with The Power of the Doctor.

Chibnall also did something groundbreaking by casting a female Doctor. This was long overdue. Imagine if they'd cast Vanessa Howard or Diana Rigg as the Doctor in the 1970s. That would have been brilliant. They probably should have done it in the 1980s. It was Chris Chibnall though who finally made the Doctor female. Now, while I personally feel that Jodie Whittaker was not very memorable as the Doctor (Jodie is excellent in other things I've seen her in but for some reason her Doctor never quite clicked for me - she often felt lightweight and miscast in the role though I did grow more fond of her near the end), it was an important step because the next time a female actor is cast as the Doctor (and it will happen) it won't be a big deal this time.

You'll have fewer people moaning next time at a female Doctor. The only people moaning will be those grim right-wing YouTube grifters who seem to have a bizarre fetish for trashing Doctor Who. If there is one thing Britain doesn't have a shortage of it is brilliant female actors. You would like to think then that the next female Doctor will be terrific. And Chris Chibnall and Jodie will be able to claim a bit of credit for that because they paved the way. Anyway, without further delay, let's take a deep dive into the Chibnall/Jodie era and go through it episode by episode. Let us examine the highs and lows of Chris Chibnall's Doctor Who...

SERIES 11

THE WOMAN WHO FELL TO EARTH (Director - Jamie Childs, Writer - Chris Chibnall)

The new Doctor crash lands in Sheffield where she will meet her new companions and tangle with an alien baddie who likes to collect the teeth of his victims. We open with Ryan Sinclair (Tosin Cole), a young man speaking on his YouTube channel (poor Ryan doesn't have that many subscribers though) about the most remarkable woman he's ever met. We think he's probably talking about the new Doctor but hold your horses for a moment because he's not. Ryan is dyspraxic (a neurological disorder which affects planning of movements and co-ordination) and so - although he's in his late teens - has not yet mastered the art of riding a bike. Chris Chibnall has a nephew who suffers from dyspraxia so (admirably) decided to write it into the show through a character to give the condition more publicity.

Ryan's dyspraxia though is what you might label inconsistent in series eleven. Chibnall soon often seems to forget that he even gave this character the condition. We see Ryan up on some hills above Sheffield trying (and failing) to ride a bike as his grandmother Grace (Sharon D Clarke) and step-grandad Graham O'Brien (Bradley Walsh) lend encouragement. This is a nice introduction to the Bradley Walsh character. There are some beautiful shots of the countryside here. These early scenes suggest that the promise of a more 'cinematic' Doctor Who has some credibility. This proves a false dawn. Despite the fancy new cameras that were much trumpeted prior to series eleven, this season often has a bland washed-out sort of look. Watch the old episodes with David Tennant during the RTD era by way of comparison. Those episodes seem much more colourful and vibrant than series eleven.

Frustrated at falling off his bike several times, Ryan throws the bike off a hill and is then quite rightly forced to go down and find it. You can't throw a perfectly nice bike off a hill. In some woodland though, Ryan encounters an alien looking orb and telephones the police. PC Yasmin Khan (Mandip Gill) duly arrives on the scene and it turns out she knew Ryan at school. Yasmin is a rather frustrated young probationary police officer in the city of Sheffield. She wants more responsibility and is eager to show what she is capable of.

It's a potentially nice idea to have a police officer as one of the Doctor's new companions. That could be quite an interesting dynamic going forward couldn't it? Well, no. The fact that Yasmin is a police officer is all but forgotten in the rest of the season. You have to feel sorry for Mandip Gill. Yasmin must be one of the most underwritten and vague regular characters in the long history of Doctor Who. She literally has no personality whatsoever. If you expected Yaz to be a charismatic companion frequently drawing on her police skills in pesky sci-fi scenarios then prepare to be disappointed.

If you asked me to write something about the Yaz character in Chibnall's series eleven of Doctor Who I would honestly struggle. About the only thing off the top of my head I remember is that Yaz had a Minnie Mouse hairstyle later on in the season. Aside from that I haven't got a huge amount of information on Yaz up my sleeve. If they edited Yaz out of most of series eleven with CGI it would make little to no difference to the plots. It's as if, at the end of the production, Chris Chibnall bumped into Mandip Gill in a BBC corridor and went "Oh, I knew I'd forgotten something! Sorry Mandip. I promise to give you some lines next year. Honestly. Remember to remind me next time."

When it comes to personality we have to say that - sadly - Ryan isn't much better than Yaz. Tosin Cole (who seems to struggling somewhat with a Yorkshire accent) often appears to be half asleep as Ryan. It's like they slipped a sedative into his cocoa and pushed him onto the set. Tosin has what can you only describe as a rather wooden and flat acting style. For all I know, Tosin might be great in his other stuff. He might be Laurence Olivier on the stage. All I can say is that, as Ryan, Tosin Cole brings the energy and acting range of a waxwork dummy to this show. One thinks of how quickly Pearl Mackie established Bill Potts as a likeable and opinionated foil for Peter Capaldi. In comparison to Mackie, Cole and Mandip are about as charismatic as a bag of bones.

Let's swiftly move on to the other characters then. Thankfully, this series does at least have Bradley Walsh as Graham. Walsh is not exactly a genius in the thesping stakes but he has an easygoing charisma and comic timing that places him head and shoulders above the rest of this cast - including, I'm sad to say, Jodie Whittaker as the Doctor. Graham is easily the most interesting and likeable character in series eleven and that's because of Bradley Walsh. Walsh does all that is asked of him in series eleven. He's the only person in this cast who deserves to be in a much better version of Doctor Who.

Back to the plot of The Woman Who Fell to Earth now. Graham and Sharon find themselves on a train which is subject to strange inexplicable events. Mysterious bundles of lightning electricity. The special effects are perfectly decent here and it's quite nice to have a horror sequence on a train at night. So far so good. The Woman Who Fell to Earth has made a solid enough start. This is not earth shattering stuff. It isn't the most exciting of the 'new Doctor' episodes we've had since 2005 but it is competent enough. It is passable. Jodie Whittaker then crashes into the train carriage as the Doctor.

The quick burst of the Doctor Who theme that heralds her entrance is a somewhat unnecessary and naff addition to this scene. Whittaker is doing the familiar (and by now rather tiresome) routine of all new Doctors in their first episode. Acting all confused and erratic because of the recent regeneration. What usually happens then though is that the Doctors settle down and then their characteristics and personality comes to the fore. By the end of the debut episode we usually have an idea of how an actor is going to play the part.

This never quite happens with Jodie though. By the end of The Eleventh Hour, Matt Smith is unquestionably the Doctor. By the end of Deep Breath, Peter Capaldi has taken command of the role. David Tennant had you accepting him as the Doctor in an episode where he spent most of the story asleep in a dressing gown! Jodie is somewhat different. By the end of this episode the jury is still slightly out but she certainly hasn't made a negative impression yet. That will come later. That's one of the bizarre things about series eleven. Jodie gives her best performance in this debut episode and then quickly gets worse as the season wears on. You'd think it would be the other way around wouldn't you? She doesn't though completely establish herself as the Doctor in the way that the previous actors were able to relatively early. She's always playing 'catch up' and never quite manages to nail the part down and make it her own.

The regeneration 'confusion' makes it difficult at this stage to get a handle on how Jodie is going to play the role but the first impressions are decent enough. She's mysterious (a quality she will quickly lose - much to the detriment of the season and Jodie) and has a sense of humour (of sorts). All Doctor traits. What helps Whittaker a lot in this first episode is that she spends most of it wearing Peter Capaldi's clothes. This oversized dark suit makes her costume look very Doctor-rish. She looks much more like the Doctor in this suit than she does in her 'official' costume (which she changes into later). You can't helped but feel slightly cheated though by the fact that Chibnall never really resolved the cliffhanger of Whittaker's regeneration when the TARDIS seemed to eject her and she was last seen falling through the sky. What happened afterwards? Well, nothing really. She landed on a train. Are Time Lords invulnerable post-regeneration?

Anyway, back to the alien stuff that Ryan encountered. The orb is revealed as a mass of biological data-gathering coils. The big villain is Tzim-Sha (Samuel Oatley) of the warlike Stenza.

The Stenza are rather obvious rip-offs of Stan Winston's Predator. They are intergalactic hunters who collect the teeth of their victims to decorate their faces. A nice macabre touch but - even so - the Stenza are not exactly the most terrifying or memorable of aliens.

You aren't exactly desperate to ever see them again after this episode. I can't be the only person who felt Tzim-Sha was more like a comedy Red Dwarf villain than a suitable foe for the Doctor. Chris Chibnall promised that series eleven would eschew established villains in favour of new ones. He's good on his word. But here's the problem - Chris Chibnall is absolutely terrible at coming up with new villains. He couldn't come up with an iconic villain to save his life. As a consequence, series eleven has no memorable villains whatsoever. Doctor Who without memorable villains is like hot water without tea. It just doesn't work.

The Doctor refers to Tzim-Sha as "Tim Shaw". It's mildly amusing. That's the sort of thing the Doctor would do. Deflate a villain through humour. The Doctor, separated from the TARDIS, must construct her own sonic from spare parts and spoons. This montage is diverting enough. The idea of this Doctor being a 'tinkerer' is fine and at this early stage of series eleven, Segun Akinola's music is interesting by virtue of being very different from what came before. The Woman Who Fell to Earth is what you might call 'ok' or 'solid' up to and around this time. It's a base from which the rest of the episode and indeed season eleven as a whole can develop. But nothing ever does develop. The most damning criticism of series eleven is that it never really gets any better than The Woman Who Fell to Earth. This is a middling but passable sort of episode and yet Chibnall's Doctor Who never actually gets better than this in series eleven. It actually gets worse. A lot worse.

At some point in The Woman Who Fell to Earth you start to think 'This is ok but when is the episode going to get exciting? What are the surprises are going to be?' Well, the episode never really becomes exciting and there are no surprises. We knew that Grace was going to die because she wasn't promoted as one of the companions in the publicity. No surprise there then. The Doctor faces off with Tim Shaw on a crane and we see the first hint that Chris Chibnall's clunky dialogue is not going to be a picnic for poor Jodie. "I'm glad you asked that again. Bit of adrenaline, dash of outrage, and a hint of panic knitted my brain back together. I know exactly who I am! I'm the Doctor, sorting out fair play throughout the universe." Chibnall is great at writing dialogue that sounds a lot better on paper than it does coming out of the mouth of an actor.

There are a number of odd moments in this episode that don't really feel like they belong in Doctor Who. The drunk man throwing salad from his kebab at Tim Shaw. The comedy relief character who listens to motivational tapes also feels like someone who could easily have been jettisoned. The Woman That Fell to Earth has what you might describe as a downbeat sort of last act with the death of Grace and the funeral. Ryan mopes about his missing dad failing to turn up and we learn that Graham only met Grace because she was his nurse when he had cancer. It's not exactly the most fun episode of Doctor Who. Get used to this. Doctor Who is rarely going to be fun in series eleven.

Chibnall's style in series eleven is more grounded and 'worthy' than his predecessors. Unfortunately, Chibnall's style here makes for a rather bland version of Doctor Who. It feels like a reheated RTD without the wit and grand arcs. What Chibnall has basically done is mimic the vague RTD blueprint but taken all the good stuff out. Chibnall's Who in series eleven is like eating a Snickers bar that has no peanuts or caramel. After the Doctor has picked out her new costume (in what seems to be a charity shop) she rigs up some alien tech to teleport off in search of her elusive TARDIS. However, a mix-up means that Ryan, Yasmin, and Graham, end up being teleported with her. This is a pretty decent cliffhanger. At this early stage in series eleven you assume that this is the approach Chibnall will take in the season. Cliffhanger endings and maybe a search through the universe for the TARDIS. That actually sounds quite exciting. Sadly though this wasn't the approach he took. You'll get no more cliffhangers from series eleven.

Jodie's costume is pretty awful. She looked much better in Capaldi's clothes. That's a great shot by the way of the Doctor looking down on Ryan as he tries to ride his bike up on the hill. In this single shot the Doctor seems mysterious, kind, and wise. She's like a cosmic guardian angel looking down on Ryan. There is so much promise in this shot that is never followed through on. This is the only time that Jodie's Doctor ever suggests an inner life in series eleven. She is silent and observing in a very Doctor-rish outfit. This is a 'what might have been' sort of moment. If only they could have made Jodie's Doctor more like this. More mysterious and aloof. More intriguing.

The last image is of the Doctor and her new companions floating in space. It feels like this is the moment where their adventures will really begin. So we give The Woman That Fell to Earth a pass. We give Jodie a pass. It's a competent if sometimes dour sixty or so minutes of television but there are sparks of promise and it feels like a relatively sturdy launching pad for the new series. Jodie's version of the Doctor is sure, we assume, to grow in stature in the forthcoming episodes and these companions will be fleshed out too. That was the assumption. The actual reality was quite different.

The end of this episode has a moment that - in hindsight - probably told us all we needed to know about Chibnall's Doctor Who. All of the guest stars in the new series are featured in a pompous 'coming soon' sort of trailer. The most laughable thing about this smug self-satisfied promo is that you've probably never heard of half of these actors. Steven Moffat managed to get people like John Hurt, Maisie Williams, and Richard E Grant in Doctor Who but he never made such a big song and dance about it.

The Woman Who Fell to Earth is a solid launch for the new era of Doctor Who. Jodie doesn't immediately nail the part in the way some of her predecessors did but shows some signs of promise. The Woman Who Fell to Earth is competent with some nice moments and images but does feel a little too downbeat for it own good at times and more akin to a traditional ITV drama than a rompish sci-fi show. At this very early stage the jury is still out on Chibnall and the new Doctor but nonetheless this was a decent start.

THE GHOST MONUMENT (Director - Mark Tonderai, Writer - Chris Chibnall)

In this episode, the Doctor, Ryan, Yaz, and Graham find themselves on a dusty barren planet called Desolation. They end up with two pilots - Angstrom (Susan Lynch) and Epzo (Shaun Dooley) - who are competing in some sort of intergalactic race. The race involves them reaching a finish point called the Ghost Monument. The mysterious organiser of the race is called Ilin (and played by Art Malik). Llin communicates with them through a holographic device.

First things first. The new titles are great. One of the best things about Chibnall's Doctor Who. So, we've got the introduction to the new Doctor and companions episode out of the way so surely The Ghost Monument is going to be a bit more fun right? Chibnall has had plenty of time to think about about Doctor Who in the months leading up to production. Surely this lifelong Doctor Who fan has plenty of great ideas and exciting plots up his sleeve? Well, no. The Ghost Monument is the episode where the alarm bells start to make themselves heard. Chris Chibnall has nothing up his sleeve in series eleven. Chibnall's version of Doctor Who is like a fancy box with ribbons on it. You open the box and there is nothing inside. It is completely empty.

The Ghost Monument was shot on location in South Africa and looks quite good. The cinematography is excellent and the idea of an intergalactic race also sounds exciting doesn't it? Unfortunately this idea doesn't translate into an entertaining episode of Doctor Who. Most of the episode consists of the characters slowly walking across a desert type environment. You'll be getting no intergalactic race capers in this snoozefest. We are told that the planet is full of deadly biological elements and hazards. We see absolutely no evidence of this in the story that follows. It is one of the most boring 49 minutes of television you are ever likely to encounter. 'Show don't tell' is a familiar piece of advice to writers. Chris Chibnall is more of a 'Tell don't show' writer in series eleven.

Early on this episode, the Doctor is picked up by a spacecraft and must negotiate with the pilot. It is in this scene that we begin to experience for the first time an awful sinking feeling about Jodie Whittaker's casting as the Doctor. She has no gravitas or presence whatsoever in this establishing scene. Her Doctor has no charismatic authority. Worst of all is the fact that in this scene Jodie sounds like she's reading her lines off cue cards. This terrible piece of acting completely pulls us out of the story.

Another thing about Jodie Whittaker that will soon become irritating in series eleven is the way that she delivers her big speeches as if she's out of breath. What is that all about? Jodie's constant waving around her her sonic - complete with exaggerated arm movement - will also start to grate. Get used to this. It will never end.

Jodie's costume in series eleven probably doesn't do her any favours. She looked more Doctor-rish (there's that term again) in the big hooded coat she wore in the short film that announced her as the Doctor. Her coat and rainbow shirt is fine but there's just something about those short trousers and large boots. It makes her look clownish and childlike. Her Doctor conforms to the costume. She IS childlike in series eleven. Toning down the 'angry angst ridden lonely God' version of the Doctor was probably a good idea. One senses that Chibnall wanted to give the character a fresh slate and make the new Doctor a bit more friendly and approachable. That's perfectly fine.

You can't help feeling though that Chibnall went too far in the other direction and got rid of too much of the stuff that MAKES the Doctor the Doctor. Jodie Whittaker's Doctor never convinces you for a second that she's a centuries old Time Lord who has saved the universe many times. She just feels like a daft young woman from Huddersfield. There is no sense of a past or any authority with Jodie's Doctor. She's just 'nice'. Jodie's Doctor is more primary school assistant or big sister than Time Lord. The Lion's share of the blame for this clearly goes to Chris Chibnall. Whittaker's performance in series eleven is mediocre at best but what chance did she have with these scripts? She isn't given much room in these stories to put her own spin on the character.

Having so many companions is already starting to look like a bad move this early in series eleven. The problem with three companions is that there is insufficient time to give them all something to do. They frequently end up just standing behind the Doctor asking questions. The large cast also does the Doctor no favours. Jodie often feels like a supporting player in the show she is supposed to be the lead of. Jodie feels like a lightweight companion when she is supposed to be the heart of the show. I think the problem is that this is essentially what Jodie is. A supporting actor. She's a sort of 'everywoman' actor. You need more of a character actor for a part like the Doctor. You need someone too who is more naturally eccentric and charismatic than Jodie.

We see in series eleven why having one companion usually works best in Doctor Who. It means that the sole companion is allowed plenty of screen time and development. It also has a latent structural benefit in that the solitary companion is our window into the world of the Doctor. We get to know the Doctor as they do. One companion also means that the Doctor/companion dynamic is much stronger and more emotional. When past companions left the show it was always a big emotional moment. Can you imagine an episode where Ryan or Yaz leaves the show having such power? Would anyone even notice they were gone? Anyway, back to the rather vague and undercooked plot of The Ghost Monument. The Doctor deduces that the Ghost Monument is her errant TARDIS stuck in mid-phasing due to the damage it suffered. Art Malik is rather wasted as Llin and doesn't get enough screen time. We learn that the Stenza have a history with this planet. Oh cripes. Don't even think about it Chibnall. We don't want Tim Shaw back in this show.

Lest we forget, the Doctor and her companions also have an encounter with some flying tea towels called the Remnants in The Ghost Monument. Thus far, Chibnall has come up with Tim Shaw and flying tea towels as new villains. I think the Daleks and Cybermen can probably sleep soundly without fear of being supplanted in the Doctor Who pantheon of memorable baddies. Elsewhere, Ryan manages to outrun some sniper robots in an action sequence so bad and so arthritically directed that you will literally wince with embarrassment. Here's the basic problem with The Ghost Monument. It's slow and boring! This is dull television. Even the two main guest stars are boring. Shaun Dooley as Epzo is given an interminable speech at one point about how he was given harsh treatment as a child that feels completely out of place. This just comes out of nowhere and is a classic example of how Chibnall will suddenly throw a dialogue scene into Doctor Who that would be more at home in Eastenders or Casualty.

These turgid slices of domestic drama style dialogue serve only to further deflate episodes that are already boring enough as it is. There's a jarring tension between Chibnall's dour drama instincts and the fact that he's writing for a rompish sci-fi show. We are on episode two and already Chibnall is starting to look like a square peg in a round hole.

It was fine (or at least tolerable) when Chibnall just came in now and again and wrote the odd episode. Steven Moffat probably tidied up his scripts anyway. Well, now you've got seven (SEVEN!) Chibnall scripts in one season (and the special) and there is no one to tidy these scripts up or tell Chris Chibnall they are rubbish. Chris Chibnall has his hands on the wheel now. He is the boss. Watch out for those rocks up ahead. This is going to be a bumpy ride!

Jodie's Doctor is already starting to become annoying in The Ghost Monument and Ryan and Yaz are complete tabula rasas. Only Bradley Walsh is keeping this ship afloat. He should be the only companion. You could argue that he'd actually be a better Doctor than Jodie Whittaker! Who would have ever predicted that before series eleven? The game show host Bradley Walsh having more wit and authority than the actor cast as the Doctor! Incredible. We now come to the only good scene in The Ghost Monument. I would argue that this is the best scene in series eleven by some considerable distance. The Doctor and her companions are left on the planet to perish but the TARDIS begins to phase in and out. The Doctor manages to stabalise the TARDIS and runs to it on a mountain range. This is a beautiful image and the music is wonderful. It's a great moment in a season almost completely devoid of them.

We are desperate to see inside though aren't we? What delights have the production designers cooked up for us? Think of all those amazing TARDIS fan art designs. Will it be Victorian steam punk? Futuristic? I'll tell you exactly what the new TARDIS interior looks like. It looks like the Match of the Day studio. The crystals are clearly made out of plastic and there isn't room to swing a cat in there. It looks cheap and cramped. It is is an utterly abysmal TARDIS interior. Did someone actually get paid to design this interior?

The Ghost Monument is, aside from that one magical scene where the TARDIS appears, a dreadfully disappointing and dull second episode for series eleven. Nothing happens in the episode, there is no sense of drama or danger, the one action sequence is embarrassing, everything feels flat and lacking energy, the cast are not gelling yet and have no chemistry with one another, the dialogue is clunky and dull. This is simply not good enough. Series eleven needed to come out of the blocks all guns blazing. Sadly though, The Ghost Monument is enough to send anyone to sleep.

If this was a brand new show - and not called Doctor Who - you would have bailed out after The Ghost Monument and watched something else next week instead. These two episodes (especially this second one) would probably not have enticed you back. So yes, it is The Ghost Monument where the shiny facade of series eleven begins to crack. It is in this episode that we realise - as painful as it might be because we all (well, most of us) wanted series eleven to be fantastic - that Chibnall's version of Doctor Who is not very good so far. This is the second episode of the bold new dawn and already we have what feels like a filler episode. Yes, I know, they went to a real location and made it look quite nice, but where is the story? Where is the excitement? Where is the horror and danger? Where is the wit? And where is the Doctor?

There is no connection in The Ghost Monument between the viewer and what is happening onscreen. The Ghost Monument does not engage us. We feel no emotion. We are simply bored. The characters stand around and talk. And sit and talk. And stand and talk. And walk and talk. They are attacked by dish cloths. The TARDIS returns. The whole of this episode is just filler to get to the TARDIS reveal. Look, that's a great moment when the TARDIS shows up but it doesn't justify the fifty or so minutes of utter boredom you have made us endure to get there. It's like a James Bond film having two hours of people talking in a room and then ending with the pre-title stunt. This is a dreadfully dull episode that fails to expand on its interesting concept. Jodie is already beginning to look out of her depth as the Doctor and, Bradley Walsh aside, the companions are rather dull and uninteresting. That's a great moment though when the TARDIS arrives. Easily the most moving scene of series eleven.

ROSA (Director - Mark Tonderai, Writer - Malorie Blackman and Chris Chibnall)

The gang arrive in Alabama in 1955 (it seems the Doctor is having trouble getting them back to present day Sheffield) and find themselves seeking to stop time-travelling racist criminal Krasko (Joshua Bowman) from preventing Rosa Parks (Vinette Robinson) influencing the American civil rights movement. Rosa Parks was, as you know, an American activist in the civil rights movement best known for her pivotal role in the Montgomery bus boycott. Rosa Parks was born Rosa Louise McCauley in Tuskegee, Alabama, on February 4, 1913. She became active in the civil rights struggle as far back as the 1940s - her husband was a member of The National Association for the Advancement of Colored People (NAACP). She worked for the local NAACP leader Edgar Nixon and Parks and her husband were members of the League of Women Voters.

In Montgomery, Alabama, on December 1, 1955, Parks refused to obey bus driver James F. Blake's order that she give up her seat in the "colored" section to a white passenger. Because of her defiance the Montgomery Bus Boycott became an important and enduring symbol of the Civil Rights movement. "I had given up my seat before, but this day, I was especially tired," said Rosa. "Tired from my work as a seamstress, and tired from the ache in my heart. As far back as I can remember, I knew there was something wrong with our way of life when people could be mistreated because of the color of their skin."

In the 1960s Rosa Parks worked for John Conyers (who served as a U.S. Representative for Michigan from 1965 to 2017) and befriended Malcolm X. She was involved in activism and campaigned to reverse the lack of housing for black people in Detroit. Rosa Parks later founded the Detroit chapter of the Joann Little Defense Committee and co-founded the Rosa L. Parks Scholarship Foundation for college-bound high school seniors. She was widowed in the 1980s and because she was prone to donating her speaking fees to charitable causes, Rosa never had much money. She was sometimes too generous for her own good. Rosa Parks died of natural causes on October 24, 2005, at the age of 92, in her apartment on the east side of Detroit. When the apartment she had lived in was threatened with demolition an artist had it rebuilt in Germany as a Rosa Parks museum.

When Rosa died, her body was transported to Washington, D.C. and transported by a bus similar to the one in which she made her protest, to lie in honour in the rotunda of the U.S. Capitol. Since the founding of the practice in 1852, Parks was the 31st person, the first American who had not been a U.S. government official, and the second private person to be honoured in this way. She was the first woman and the second black person to lie in honour in the Capitol. Asked how she wanted to be remembered, Rosa Parks said - "I would like to be remembered as a person who wanted to be free so other people would be also free." Her defiance during the civil rights struggle and participation in activism has secured Rosa Parks a lasting legacy in history

You know that series eleven must be bad if Rosa is lauded as its stand out classic episode. This is supposed to be a great episode? Rosa is a rather dreary and dull episode where the drama comes from the shuffling around of bus time tables. Yes, bus time tables! Should Doctor Who even be tackling stories like this in the first place? You could make a case either way. Chibnall's Who is definitely what you might call 'on the nose' in terms of social issues and politics. In the classic late fifties/early sixties Twilight Zone, the great (and very liberal) Rod Serling would often address topical and important issues like race, fear of outsiders, prejudice, war, the mob mentality, conformity, censorship, and discrimination, but he would use science fiction in order to disguise these themes from the conservative television networks of the era.

Serling made his political points and delivered his social messages but did so through brilliant and entertaining stories. Sometimes though, now and again, he would be a little bit too 'on the nose' and forget to give you a good story with his themes. When Serling was a trifle too on the nose you'd get episodes like I Am the Night—Color Me Black - where in a small prejudiced town, permanent 24 hour darkness descends as a man is about to be wrongfully hung for killing a bigot in self-defence. Though well-meaning, these sorts of episodes were slow, dull, talky, and dramatically obvious.

Chibnall's Doctor Who is too often like this. You are deluged with politics and 'messages' but don't get an entertaining story through which these messages can be delivered in a natural way. Consequently, this incarnation of Doctor Who feels preachy and obvious. It feels dumbed down. Doctor Who is already hardwired with latent positive messages. The Doctor is a character who wins by brains and not brawn. The Doctor is tolerant, fights prejudice, helps people, and doesn't carry a gun. The Doctor is the ultimate outsider. Do fans of Doctor Who really need Chris Chibnall to constantly hammer them over the head with obvious politics?

One of my personal problems with Rosa is that there always feels something slightly 'off' about episodes of Doctor Who set in the United States. It just never quite feels right. It's like when American shows do an episode in Britain. Their depiction of Britain always feels like a lazy caricature and the flip reverse is true. One can't help feeling that if they'd wanted to write an episode about prejudice and racism then there are plenty of British periods in history they could have chosen rather than tackle a very American piece of history. You never even feel like the characters are really in America in Rosa. It's obvious it was part of the South African shoot.

My main complaint about Rosa is that it's a middling half decent piece of drama in its own right but a terrible episode of Doctor Who. Rosa Parks deserves more than to be a supporting character in a boring episode of Doctor Who. Write a book or make a drama about Rosa Parks instead. Quantum Leap and Star Trek both did better episodes about American racism than Doctor Who does here. That's because they were American shows. It gave them more authenticity.

There's a terrific performance by Vinette Robinson as Rosa Parks but the actual episode is incredibly dull. There's a completely unnecessary villain too (who looks like he's just wandered in from an eighties pop video) named Krasko who you feel sure must have been an addition by Chris Chibnall. If there's one thing Chris Chibnall is great at it is creating rubbish villains. Maybe this episode would have been better off as a pure historical? The fact that Krasko is a racist from the far future is an incredibly depressing subplot. You'd think the future would be more enlightened than the past. It usually is in classic sci-fi like Star Trek.

Krasko - unfortunately - again highlights the fact that Jodie Whittaker doesn't have much substance and steel to her Doctor in confrontations with the villains. She just doesn't have any sense of presence. When the policeman (who is arguably the best villain in series eleven) menaces the Doctor and Graham in their room in this episode, it is Bradley Walsh as Graham who seems to have more authority and strength - not Jodie Whittaker's Doctor. Graham feels more like the Doctor in this scene than Jodie Whittaker. That's a really awful state of affairs when a companion feels more like the Doctor than the person playing the Doctor. I've no idea why Chibnall decided to make Jodie's Doctor so weak in series eleven.

Could you imagine a scene like this where Peter Capaldi's Doctor felt weak and ineffectual compared to a companion in the face of a bully? No, you couldn't. Capaldi's Doctor actually punched a racist after the racist insulted Bill in Thin Ice. Jodie's Doctor, by contrast, often seems physically intimidated during confrontations. She shrinks into the background when she is supposed to be commanding the room and taking charge. Take the moment where the racist slaps Ryan at the start of the episode. The Doctor just looks shocked and meekly says they don't want any trouble as she edges away into the background. This is not the Doctor. The real Doctor wouldn't stand for a racist slapping one of his/her companions. When Ryan and Yaz suffer from prejudice in the cafe, the Doctor suggests they should go back to the TARDIS. It took her this long to realise that Ryan and Yaz might stand out somewhat in 1955 Alabama? Is she stupid? You'd think this Doctor had never travelled in time before.

The most baffling thing about series eleven is the way that it strips the Doctor of all the qualities that make the character so interesting and iconic. The Doctor is brilliant, enigmatic, mysterious, ancient, sometimes grumpy or rude, funny, alien, eccentric, wise, powerful, charismatic, and compassionate. All you get from Jodie's Doctor is that she's quite nice. That's it. She's nice. Jodie's Doctor doesn't seem wise, ancient, brilliant, alien, enigmatic, aloof, mysterious, or have any suggestion of an inner life or past. It makes this version of the Doctor feel bland. The 'quirky' lines that Jodie is constantly saddled with feel clumsy and clunky. She's constantly saying things like "Oh, a trampoline, I love trampolines me, I think I invented the trampoline" and it makes her Doctor seem childlike and not very bright.

The writing of Jodie's Doctor feels like an attempt to pitch her somewhere in the middle of David Tennant and Matt Smith. But these two actors had superior showrunners writing for them and were allowed to have more range in their interpretations of the Doctor. David Tennant could often be dark and Matt Smith was naturally quirky and eccentric in a way that Jodie isn't. Matt Smith was brilliant at making his Doctor feel like an ancient alien in the body of a young person. We see no evidence that Jodie is capable of any of this and - to be fair to her - she is never really even given the chance.

The scene at the end of Rosa where the Doctor educates Ryan, Yaz, and Graham about Rosa Parks as they look up at a television type screen in the TARDIS is one of the worst scenes in television history. It makes Ryan, Yaz, and Graham look like dim school children and - worst of all - it makes the Doctor appear insufferably patronising. It also exposes the dreadful TARDIS interior. They are quite patently all standing in a television studio set. It looks ridiculous! Why is there no sense of a larger TARDIS beyond this crappy interior set? We never see any evidence in series eleven that the TARDIS extends beyond this small room. In the previous series of Doctor Who it was always made apparent that this was merely the entrance to the TARDIS and the control room (so to speak).

The closing credits for this episode eschew the Doctor Who theme in favour of "Rise Up" by Andra Day. It is unnecessary touches like this that make Rosa - and series eleven as a whole - feel unbearably smug, pretentious and self-satisfied. Rosa is a well meaning episode but, with the best will in the world, this is not exactly exciting television. It doesn't feel much like Doctor Who. It feels more like a middling episode of Quantum Leap.

And the depiction of racism negates the important themes through lack of nuance. Almost every white person in the episode is a cartoon racist. The frightening thing about racism is that you don't always know what the real views of someone are in private. You could meet someone who seemed ok at first glance but not know they are a racist. The 'unmasking' of a racist who seemed affable on the surface would be more powerful than some cartoon villain slapping Ryan. Also, surely there were a few decent white people in 1955 who didn't agree with segregation and the prejudice against black people? Rosa depicts a United States where everyone is racist.

Rosa is desperate to be 'worthy' and important but if you come to Doctor Who for an entertaining ride to go with your side-helping of positive social messages then you aren't going to get much in the way of that. As the gang seek to alter the bus time tables I wondered if this was really happening. The plot of a Doctor Who episode revolving around bus time tables. It is every bit as boring as it sounds. Rosa feels like a somewhat out of place Doctor Who story to me. It made me wish that there was someone in charge of this show capable of writing a powerful and thought provoking episode about racism but through the prism of pure science fiction. Sadly, that person is never going to be Chris Chibnall. Rosa is a largely tedious episode that wastes some good supporting performances and its well intentioned message. Shouldn't Doctor Who be tackling racism is a more allegorical and entertaining way?

ARACHNIDS IN THE UK (Director - Sallie Aprahamian, Writer - Chris Chibnall)

Most of the story for Arachnids in the UK, which was the fourth episode of series eleven, takes place in an empty country hotel where a Trump analogue named Jack Robertson (Chris Noth) is overseeing the completion of a new hotel complex which has a spider problem. Earlier, now back in Sheffield, the Doctor had encountered a giant spider in the flat of one of Yaz's neighbours. Giant spiders. Well, surely even Chris Chibnall can't mess up an episode featuring giant spiders can he? This episode is bound to be fun isn't it? Sadly, Arachnids in the UK (that's a very weak pun) is a baffling and unsatisfying episode that could only have come from the pen of Chris Chibnall. Count on Chris Chibnall to make an episode featuring giant spiders dull.

Arachnids is probably the episode in this season that finally confirmed the worst fears of Doctor Who fans. This is episode four and series eleven is not getting any better. Quite the contrary. It is getting worse. Hold on tight everyone. We are now in freefall. All the problems that the first three episodes have already alerted us to are magnified in this episode. Jodie's Doctor has no charisma or authority. The companions - save for Graham - are personality vacuums. Chibnall just can't write decent villains to save his life.

There is just something weirdly 'off' about Chibnall's Doctor Who in series eleven. It feels lifeless and flat. It doesn't engage. It is boring. We are only on episode four of Chibnall's Who and already it feels like a chore to sit through rather than something we look forward to each week. Arachnids in the UK does have one highlight near the start when we see the new beautifully designed Time Vortex as the TARDIS hurtles through the universe. This is a great moment in a season largely devoid of memorable moments. If only series eleven could generate this sense of wonder more often.

Yes, as many fans pointed out, the not-Trump character was

actually more humane than the Doctor in this episode by wanting to shoot the spiders. The Doctor wanted them to suffocate in a horrible death. That's a really delightful and fun plot insertion by Chibnall isn't it? Spiders suffocating to death. Thanks for that Chris. Is he completely determined to make sure that Doctor who is no fun whatsoever to anyone? Who the hell is he writing this show for?

The scene where Ryan plays some 'banging' Grime music to entice the spiders is embarrassing enough to make you cringe. It feels like Chibnall trying to get down with the kids. Scenes like this have no place in an episode of Doctor Who. Perhaps the absolute worst thing about this episode is the way the not-Trump character never gets his comeuppance. You wait for the moment where the Doctor is inevitably going to make him look stupid or overwhelm him with the force of her intellect and personality. That moment never arrives. It's little wonder that the not-Trump character is reluctant to accept that this Doctor is in charge. You wouldn't want this version of the Doctor in charge of anything.

The CGI special effects in this episode are adequate (there isn't really enough spider carnage to really put them to the test) but there are no great moments of horror that will have kids (or adults) hiding behind the settee. You'd think that a giant spider episode might contain someone trapped in a web or about to be eaten or something purely for tension but nothing of this kind ever arrives. Think of how terrifying the giant spider scene in the Lord of the Rings trilogy was. Eighties films with old school effects like Krull have scarier giant spider scenes than Arachnids in the UK.

This episode continues the strange inability of Chibnall to give Yaz anything to do. She's a police officer right? This is her home patch. You'd assume she would assert some sort of authority in this episode but she never does. This is a really boring and unsatisfying episode ultimately. If you are expecting a fun romp where giant spiders invade Sheffield and the Doctor saves the day with a brilliant piece of ingenuity then I'm afraid you are going to be disappointed. The spider capers are dull and rationed, the Doctor is ineffectual and bland, and by the end of Arachnids in the UK you'll never have any good reason to ever watch this episode again.

It really does take a special brand of ineptness to decide to have a giant spider story and then make it this boring. Chibnall obviously decided that series eleven needed a bit of a romp at this stage to liven it up and give the viewer more variety and in that he was correct. Series eleven does need a bit more fun at this stage. However the B-movie romp that you expect from Arachnids never arrives. This is unforgivably dull stuff with terrible dialogue, plot threads that vanish into think air, a main cast that still don't have any chemistry with one another, terrible attempts at humour, an obvious message about toxic waste that feels like it was tacked on as an afterthought, and a general plot that makes no sense whatsoever. If you were in charge of Doctor Who and someone sent you this script in the post you'd throw it in the waste paper bin.

Chibnall never even bothered to write an ending for this episode. It just fizzles out. There is no particular reason for the not-Trump character to be in this episode (guest star Chris Noth genuinely seems to have no idea what he is even acting in here and you can hardly blame him) and it's starting to get slightly tiresome the way Chibnall keeps giving the Doctor anti-gun speeches. You don't need to keep telling us this as if you are the only person in the world in possession of this knowledge. Guns are bad, prejudice is wrong, Donald Trump is a buffoon. We get it. We know. We AGREE with you. You don't need you to constantly keep telling us this stuff as if we are stupid. It just makes your version of Doctor Who feel patronising.

You'd expect Jodie to be settling into the role of the Doctor by now and putting her own stamp on the character. If anything the opposite is true. In this episode Jodie is often literally reduced to gurning and pulling funny faces. Chibnall constantly has her reciting dialogue too that feels like rejected leftovers from an old Matt Smith script. "Look at your views! Never had a flat. I should get a one, I'd be good in a flat. I could get a sofa. Imagine me with a sofa, like my own sofa. I could get a purple one and sit on it..." The contrived 'I'm mad I am!' aspect to Jodie's Doctor is not only unconvincing it's already tiresome and annoying.

All the problems we've had already detected in Chibnall's Who are doubled-down on with a vengeance here. Too much expositional dialogue, too much clunky dialogue, a dull one note villain, no ending or twists, a dull story, lack of energy, dull direction, no sense of threat, a Doctor that feels more like an annoying companion than the Doctor. The charm, wit, imagination and surprises of Doctor Who are all gone. At this stage in series eleven, Chibnall has sucked the heart out of this show. He has made it boring.

Arachnids in the UK is bizarre in the way that it has no structure. It feels like a bunch of random scenes have been cut together in the wrong order. The plot threads left dangling from this episode should form part of a screenwriting module. It's like Chibnall started writing a giant spider episode and then lost interest after twenty pages.

Arachnids in the UK is just terrible. Dull, preachy, tedious, a cast who aren't gelling together, awful dialogue, plot threads that vanish into thin air, an irritating and ineffectual Doctor. This is dismal unacceptable stuff. Arachnids in the UK is an unfinished script played by a cast who all look like they'd rather be somewhere else.

THE TSURANGA CONUNDRUM (Director - Jennifer Perrott, Writer - Chris Chibnall)

The Doctor and her 'fam' set off a sonic mine at a space Junkyard (or something like that) and wake aboard the Tsuranga, an automated ship travelling to a medical space-station. There are a bunch of uninteresting characters on the ship but also a Pting - a small Gremlin like alien which eats through metal. The start of this episode has the Doctor and her companions sifting through a rubbish dump. It feels like a metaphor for series eleven. Maybe they are looking for a decent script? The Tsuranga Conundrum, which was the fifth episode of series eleven, is one of the worst episodes of Doctor Who ever made. It is a title in search of a story. The episode consists almost entirely of Jodie Whittaker walking up and down a couple of corridors, waving her arms around and endlessly explaining the almost non-existent plot on a loop.

This was clearly a 'budget' episode designed to save money. If you are looking for entertainment and spectacle you've come to the wrong place. Go and watch something else. At one point in The Tsuranga Conundrum there is a space battle. Sounds fun right? Sadly, the space battle is conveyed by someone standing in a room in a virtual reality device. Seriously? Look, I know Doctor Who under Chris Chibnall not have an unlimited budget up its sleeve. I get that. But special effects are relatively easy to get hold of these days. You can get good effects on a modest budget. The Steve Moffat era of Doctor Who had some space opera. He didn't have a huge amount of money to juggle either.

The Tsuranga Conundrum is like a special expert masterclass in how not to write a Doctor Who story. The premise is dull, the 'villain' is dull, the location is dull, the supporting characters are dull, nothing happens, there is no tension, it is all 'tell don't show', the companions have nothing to do. Even the Doctor is dull.

Chibnall gives the Doctor a bizarre speech in the middle of this episode about how she loves science. It feels completely out of place. It's like Chibnall read something in an encyclopedia or saw a quote he liked and so shoehorned it into the episode through a speech the Doctor makes. "The particle accelerator smashes the atoms together, like a little anti-matter factory, to produce positrons, which are then stored very carefully inside electric and magnetic fields. The positrons interact with the fuel materials to produce heat, which produces thrust. It's beautiful. Anti-matter powering the movement of matter. Bringing positrons into existence to move other forms of life across space. I love it. Conceptually, and actually."

Chris Chibnall's dialogue sounds like it's gone through a google translation filter from Slovak. You can see Jodie Whittaker visibly grappling with this clunky 'science' dialogue and trying to make it sound natural but she can't. It isn't natural and she's not good enough to disguise this. Hasn't Chris Chibnall worked out yet that Jodie isn't very good at this sort of stuff? He cast her. Chibnall's habit of having the Doctor constantly explain everything as if her companions are ten years-old makes Jodie's character incredibly irritating. Who'd want to travel through space with this patronising charisma vacuum?

The Pting must be the worst alien in any episode of Doctor Who ever. Notice how it eats through anything but leaves the lame android alone. This CGI creature is vaguely Gremlin like and absolutely preposterous. This creature is the size of a teddy bear but Jodie Whittaker looks terrified and flinches when she confronts it. This Doctor is literally scared of her own shadow. Why is Chibnall writing the first female Doctor as a wimp? Wouldn't it be more progressive to have the first female Doctor be bold and confident? A touch of arrogance even?

It feels like Chibnall decided to have a woman Doctor but then couldn't really work out how he was going to write a woman Doctor so he just ignored the gender change and decided to make this new Doctor nicer and less aloof than we are used to. Isn't this a bit patronising from Chibnall? He casts the first woman ever to play the Doctor and the only personality trait he gives her is to be a bit skittish and nice (in a bland sort of way)?

Christopher Eccleston is often described as an actor who was great at the serious angry Doctor scenes but somewhat out of his comfort zone with the quirky humourous stuff. There's maybe an element of truth in that but Eccleston got plenty of good dialogue and some powerful scenes to sink his teeth into. Russell T Davies played to Eccleston's strengths often enough to make him a memorable Doctor. Jodie Whittaker was required to be play the Doctor in series eleven as a daffy primary school teacher. It is the blandest and least memorable interpretation of the Doctor we have ever experienced. But was that her fault? What was she supposed to do with these scripts?

Even though this ship in The Tsuranga Conundrum is supposed to be in grave danger you get no sense of that watching the episode. The characters wander around in lackadaisical fashion with no sense of urgency or threat. The resolution to the threat is classic Chibnall in its underwhelming nature. It literally feels like he just makes these endings up off the top of his head as they shoot the episode. It's like Chibnall turns in his Doctor Who scripts with the last act missing and then just cobbles something together on the spot as they near the end of the shoot.

The subplot of the pregnant man in this episode is also classic Chibnall. What is the point of this character? Chibnall thinks this is an amusing subplot but it isn't funny in the least. The actor playing the pregnant man is insufferable. Ryan's speech to the man about caring for his child has the obvious subtext of Ryan's missing father. But I don't care about Ryan's missing father. I don't even care about Ryan. If Ryan got sucked out of an airlock in this episode I don't think I would have even noticed he was missing the next week when the new episode aired.

Ryan's speech to the annoying pregnant man is another classic example of how Chibnall will drop a 'dramatic' scene into the middle of Doctor Who that feels like it was written for Holby City or Eastenders. We have never experienced such a jarring disconnect before between the show and the showrunner as we do in series eleven.

There is an incant service at the end of this episode which the Doctor insists on joining. "May the saints of all the stars and constellations bring you hope as they guide you out of the dark and into the light on this voyage and the next, and all the journeys still to come." Pass the vomit bag. What is this nonsense? Someone please unplug Chris Chibnall's computer. He makes Mark Gattis look like Dostoevsky. This is another Chris Chibnall script that should be on a roaring fire turning into ashes rather than fogging up our television screens and boring everyone to death.

There is just no excuse for episodes like this. The Tsuranga Conundrum makes Eaters of the Light look like The Empire Strikes Back. The Tsuranga Conundrum is lamentable stuff. Absolutely tedious, chock full of wooden acting, one of the worst scripts in the history of human civilisation, a laughable alien villain, no pacing, no structure, no drama, no wit, no emotion, no fun, no excitement, no magic. It's hard to think of many worse episodes since the show came back in 2005. In fact, I could only think of ONE myself but we'll have to wait for series twelve for that.

DEMONS OF THE PUNJAB (Director - Jamie Childs, Writer - Vinay Patel)

Yaz asks the Doctor to take her to see her grandmother (Leena Dhingra) when her grandmother (now Amita Suman) was young. They end up in the Punjab in 1947 and the Doctor soon deduces that aliens are present. But what is the motive of these mysterious aliens? The partition of India is conveyed in this episode by a few sheds in the middle of nowhere. This is a Yaz-centric episode. God knows if anyone needed a spotlight it was poor Yaz. However, at the conclusion of this episode she still hasn't really come into her own right as a character much more. Graham and Ryan get virtually nothing to do in this episode. These must be the most underwritten companions in

Doctor Who history.

Demons of the Punjab an improvement over the Chibnall episodes we've endured so far in series eleven - with the exception of The Woman Who Fell to Earth. The Woman Who Fell to Earth was not exactly classic Doctor Who but it was reasonably solid and interesting in a way that the rest of the season isn't. Demons of the Punjab is better than the previous three episodes (yes, even Rosa - an episode I contend is dull despite its positive reception) but that really isn't saying much. It's not exactly a high bar to clear.

Demons of the Punjab still though has many of the same problems that have dogged most of series eleven. The most salient problem is that, like most of series of eleven, Demons of the Punjab is mostly boring and the acting is abysmal. There is really no excuse for making a season of Doctor Who this boring. And yet, Chris Chibnall seemed to think this was a tremendously exciting show when he was promoting it on the publicity junket. Yes, I know, he's not going to say anything else. He's not going to go - "Yeah, I'd lower your expectations this year. I've watched it and, to be honest, it's really boring. I expect a lot of people will fall asleep trying to watch this." The thing is though, I genuinely believe sometimes that series eleven is Chibnall's idea of a good show.

The sci-fi elements in Demons feel like an afterthought but they do at least prevent us from completely falling asleep. The Thijarians have a vague Cenobite/Hellraiser sort of look which is quite good fun but the episode fizzles out somewhat when they are revealed to be benign aliens who are simply here to commemorate people who have died alone. I'm sure it wasn't intentional but they feel like a vague rip-off of the Testimony from Twice Upon a Time (and that story was only a handful of episodes ago).

The twist that the aliens are not a threat means that Demons of the Punjab continues one of the many weaknesses of series eleven in that there is never any sense of threat or danger for the characters. None of the situations the Doctor and her companions find themselves in during series eleven have any tension. These aren't compelling situations. Consequently, the episodes, whatever their merit (or lack of) as pieces of drama, fall flat and become a chore to watch. Never before in Doctor Who have you glanced at your watch so many times wondering how much longer an episode has to run as you so frequently do in series eleven.

We get a rarity in Demons of the Punjab. Graham and Yaz actually have a conversation! This cast are still not gelling though. There is no great chemistry fizzing around in their interactions. Tosin Cole and Mandip Gill often feel like members of the public who have won some sort of competition to appear in an episode of Doctor Who and Jodie continues to present the blandest incarnation of the Doctor we have ever seen. She is simply bringing nothing to this part in series eleven. It feels like Jodie's entire research for this iconic role consisted of watching ten minutes of a Matt Smith or David Tennant episode.

There's a death in this episode near the end that continues the weird downbeat aura that has filtered through series eleven. What makes this worse is the fact that the Doctor decides she can't intervene and just wanders away. It compounds the sense of this Doctor being weak and useless. One other thing about Demons of the Punjab which reminds you of Chibnall's episodes is the way that this story just seems to sort of fizzle out in the end. Series eleven is very strange in the way that these episodes feel like first drafts that were rushed into production. None of these stories feel complete or satisfying.

One other glaring problem with series eleven is the way that these episodes feel padded out. The running time of episodes in series eleven has been extended (at the cost of a shorter run of ten episodes) and the scripts are struggling with this. Few of these stories in series eleven have enough substance to them to justify the extra length. And worst of all is that these stories are unforgivably dull and boring! Where is the excitement and fun? Where is the wit? Where are the twists and surprises? Demons of the Punjab is like some tepid 'worthy' drama with the Doctor and a sci-fi subplot thrown in as an afterthought.

The guest stars in this episode are pretty hopeless and bland. Alongside the regular wooden performances of Jodie, Tosin, and Mandip, there is practically a forest of teak onscreen in Demons of the Punjab. You could take Jodie's Doctor out of these episodes and we wouldn't miss her in the slightest. If anything, these episodes are more of a drag when Jodie is front and centre, pulling funny faces, pointing her sonic around as if her arm is stuck, and rattling off subpar Tennant whimsy.

Demons of the Punjab is not as bad as some of the stuff Chibnall has written (how could anything be that bad?) in series eleven but it still isn't good enough, not by a long shot. It's still bland and sort of forgettable. If this had been in series ten, you'd think of it as that boring episode set in India where nothing much happened that you had to sit through on the way to the big two part finale.

Like most of series eleven, you'll have no good reason to ever sit through Demons of the Punjab again. It is absolutely unacceptable that this shortened season of ten episodes has so many dull stories where nothing much happens. You'd have thought that a shorter than usual season would be an advantage. You'd have thought this would make it easier to stretch the budget and avoid too many filler episodes. The reverse is - sadly - the case though. We have the worst of all possible worlds in series eleven. A shortened season that is almost entirely composed of dull filler episodes. The lack of ambition in this shortened season is quite unforgivable.

KERBLAM! (Director - Jennifer Perrott, Writer - Pete McTighe)

The Doctor and her companions travel to Kerblam!, a galaxy-wide online shopping service consisting of automated warehouses, and a mostly robotic workforce known as "TeamMates". Under the guise of being new employees, the group attempt to find out who had sent them a delivery with a call for help. This episode takes place in a very exciting location. A warehouse. It's not even a futuristic warehouse most of the time. It is literally a bog standard warehouse with racking of the sort that many people will have worked in. The plot evokes Paradise Towers and the Happiness Patrol. Kerblam! seems to be a series eleven episode that many fans thought was sort of alright. At the very least it is a more lighthearted 'caper' than some of the other episodes we've endured and we don't feel as if we are endlessly being bashed over the head with a platitudinous political commentary.

Bizarrely though, the message of the story seems to be the Doctor siding with capitalism over the workers. That's a rather odd development! The Doctor is way too excited at the start for my tastes when she has a visit from the Kerblam man (or whatever it was). Why would the Doctor get into a childlike fit of excitement over some capitalist corporation? You couldn't imagine Capaldi acting like that. It seems almost cruel sometimes the way that Jodie came straight after Capaldi. We went from probably the best actor to ever play the part to someone who pulls funny faces. Talk about the sublime to the ridiculous.

The big guest star is that comedy titan Lee Mack. Sarcasm aside, Lee Mack doesn't get much to do. You do get the always terrific Julie Hesmondhalgh though as a manager named Judy Maddox. One problem with Kerblam! is that it looks like a rather cheap episode at the best of times. They obviously saved money by just shooting most of this in a real ordinary warehouse. It's not the most arresting of locations. The Doctor and her gang pretending to be workers is rather risible (I've worked in a warehouse and I can assure you that you aren't allowed to just stand around and chit chat all day!) but the robots in this are quite good fun and sort of creepy. It's the first time that series eleven has successfully managed to be creepy.

Sadly, a lot of the problems that have plagued series eleven are still apparent though. The direction and pacing of the episodes in this season has been disappointingly flat and dull and that trend continues here. Kerblam! lacks energy and never really grabs the audience. The writer of this episode is perhaps not at fault as he's written a chase scene and a big confrontation. It's not his fault that the episode is directed in such a staid fashion. I suspect that Pete McTighe probably imagined his warehouse to be more overtly futuristic too. He must have been disappointed when he saw how cheap the episode looked on the screen.

The main cast members are still a big problem. Bradley Walsh is doing his thing, which is fine because he's funny and likeable, but Ryan and Yaz are still absolutely terrible. You'd think Tosin and Mandip had never acted in their lives by the way they deliver some of their lines. Jodie's Doctor continues to be lightweight and forgettable. When she confronts the villain it is always laughable because she has no authority or presence. When Capaldi, Tennant, Eccleston or Smith had to confront a villain it was always riveting because they were capable of showing how powerful and dangerous the Doctor could be. Jodie just can't seem to do that. In series eleven she often looks frightened when she has to confront someone.

This is the 'supply teacher' version of the Doctor. And it's not because of her gender. Could you imagine if someone like Jodie Comer or Michelle Gomez was playing the Doctor? If they had to threaten a villain it would be spellbinding and scary. Jodie's lack of gravitas and authority is a recurring problem with series eleven. The worst thing about season eleven is that you feel like the other actors (whoever they were) who might have been in the frame to play the Doctor must have considered it a lucky escape when they saw the actual show that Chibnall had made. It's hard to think of any actor, however brilliant, who could have consistently kept their head above water in a show this boring and badly written. A young

Diana Rigg would have struggled to breathe life into this season let alone poor Jodie.

There's a big chase sequence in this episode featuring conveyor belts. The special effects are dodgy to say the least and it doesn't have much suspense. Ryan's dyspraxia seems to come and go in series eleven. Sometimes he has it and at other times it's as if Chris Chibnall completely forgot he'd given Ryan this condition in the first place. Kerblam! is sort of like a forgettable Russell T Davies/Tennant era episode. You could imagine Davies doing an episode like this and it would be passable enough - if hardly the most memorable of Doctor Who stories. Kerblam! is better than some of the more dismal episodes in season eleven but it's no great shakes all the same. Anyone hoping for a massive upturn in quality for series eleven to have arrived by now is going to be disappointed.

When I sat down to write something about Kerblam! I racked my brain and found that I could remember almost nothing about the episode. I last watched Listen years ago and yet can remember almost everything that happens in that episode. I haven't watched Heaven Sent for a while but know the episode by heart. I haven't watched some of the Christopher Eccleston episodes for years but I could easily write about that season off the top of my head if I had to. Kerblam! though, I can barely remember at all. Kerblam! did not lodge itself in my memory. It had no great moments that I can recall in an instant. The plot and characters washed over me. They went in and straight back out again. Nothing in the episode stayed with me.

And that's the problem with series eleven. It doesn't register. It doesn't affect you. You feel no connection to anything that is happening. All eras of Doctor Who have had forgettable episodes that you don't feel in a rush to watch again. It's probably unavoidable. Very few television shows are consistently brilliant from week to week. Series eleven is unique though in the way that nearly every episode is forgettable. Would anyone seriously sit down and ever watch these episodes again? They were bad enough the first time around. Kerblam! is at least a bit lighter and more fun than the early episodes of series eleven but it's still completely forgettable all the same.

THE WITCHFINDERS (Director - Sallie Aprahamian, Writer - Joy Wilkinson)

In this series eleven episode, the Doctor and her companions end up in 17th century Lancashire where a witch trial is taking place. The Doctor pretends to be the Witchfinder General and matters are complicated by King James (Alan Cumming) turning up. As you can probably guess, the Doctor might be taken for a witch herself before this particular adventure has ended. This is an episode that many people were looking forward to when they saw the episode titles for season eleven. Well, this one was bound to be fun wasn't it? Maybe a rompish riff on Hammer films? The Doctor and the gang at a 17th century witch trial sounds like a can't miss idea. It's another wasted opportunity though. The budget for this episode is so non existent that they don't even have horses. King James has no entourage!

Guest star Alan Cumming hams his part to oblivion. His voice is apparently based on Malcolm Rifkind. Cumming's archness is a rather cruel counter point to the rest of the cast - Jodie, Mandip, and Tosin in particular. Cumming seems to have deduced that this episode isn't very good so he's just going to have fun. Cumming is not much of an actor but he does have a presence and a flamboyant scenery chewing sort of campy charisma. So when he is acting with Jodie it magnifies the fact that she is lacking these qualities. She doesn't have any charisma or comic timing. She is blown off the screen when she has to act with Cumming. When you watch their scenes together you unavoidably keep thinking that Alan Cumming would be a better Doctor than Jodie.

David Tennant managed to hold his own with Catherine Tate - who is a famous comedian in real life. Peter Capaldi managed to compete with Michelle Gomez - who is literally a force of nature. Matt Smith was an equal in his sparring with the larger than life River Song - played by an over the top Alex Kingston. Faced with a similar challenge, Jodie Whittaker just fades into the background. She is often the dullest person in a show where she is supposed to be the lead.

There's a ludicrous moment in this episode where the Doctor gets into a huff and declares that if she was a 'bloke' everyone would be listening to her. It doesn't make much sense because she's already convinced these people that she is the Witchfinder General and had numerous conversations with everyone! Also, why does no one seem to notice the anachronistic clothes of the Doctor and her companions? Why don't they ever wear period clothes from the TARDIS wardrobe in series eleven? The Doctor complaining about sexist attitudes in The Witchfinders doesn't make any sense. Does she not know she's in the 17th century? What does she expect? You'd think the Doctor would have visited this period before.

Another inconsistent aspect to this incarnation of the Doctor is the way she insists they can't intervene at fixed points in history but then breaks her own rules when the plot calls for it. These details compound the fact that Jodie's Doctor doesn't really have a distinct personality or character. She's just there waving her arms around dispensing (mostly awful) rapid fire dialogue. There is a bizarre refusal by the writing in series eleven to let Jodie play the Doctor we know. This is essentially a brand new character that has little to do with the established Doctor. You don't even feel like Jodi is an alien. She just feels like an ordinary human woman who has borrowed the TARDIS for a spin-off show while we wait for the real Doctor to return. This is basically what series eleven feels like. A forgettable CBBC Doctor Who spin-off show. The Sarah Jane Adventures was vastly superior to this rubbish.

There's a great missed opportunity in this episode when the Doctor is a prisoner and has an exchange with King James about their true nature. He points out that she too hides behind her name. It's a fascinating moment and one of the few times in series eleven that Jodi's Doctor suggests an inner life as she contemplates this assertion. What happens next? Absolutely nothing! They go nowhere with this and that's series eleven in a nutshell. It's just an empty, hollow, bland season of television. There is no subtext or mystery to this show. There is no ambition to anything in series eleven. No grand plan or arc.

Doctor Who wasn't always perfect with Steven Moffat but you knew it was a labour of love for him. You knew he was throwing the kitchen sink at the show. Series eleven feels like a show made by people who just see this as their latest job and want these episodes finished as quickly as possible so they can go home and do something else. There is no enthusiasm to anything. No energy or creativity. Series eleven is completely stale. It feels dull and tired.

It's interesting to compare this episode with the Inside No. 9 story The Trial of Elizabeth Gadge. I can assure you that Inside No. 9 has less money up its sleeve than Doctor Who but they still did a 17th century witch trial story more convincingly. The Trial of Elizabeth Gadge was not only witty in the way that it juxtaposed the preposterous nature of witch trial evidence with the grave formality of the trials but it was also beautifully acted and had the great David Warner. It even had a horror twist at the end. The Trial of Elizabeth Gadge had a funny and clever script and memorable characters. All that The Witchfinders ultimately has going for it is Alan Cumming hamming it up and doing a silly voice to amuse himself.

The Witchfinders also does that familiar series eleven thing of throwing some nonsense about aliens in at the last minute - thus leading to a climax that is oddly similar to the flying tea towels from The Ghost Monument. The decent performance of Siobhan Finneran as Becka Savage in The Witchfinders and the broad but entertaining antics of Alan Cumming do - unfortunately - throw yet more negative shade onto Tosin Cole and Mandip Gill. Ryan and Yaz are surely two of the dullest companions in the history of Doctor Who. Even good old Bradley Walsh is starting a look bit bored by this stage and who can blame him? Having three companions continues to be a problem in series eleven that the writing can't seem to adjust to.

And yet, in series ten we had episodes where the Doctor had Bill, Nardole and Missy as companions in the TARDIS and it worked fine. All were unique characters in their own right, all of them had something to do, and Capaldi's Doctor was still a strong undiminished presence at the heart of it all. Moffat was able to juggle four characters in the TARDIS. Chibnall's version of Doctor Who can't even get the Doctor right let alone juggle a crowded TARDIS team.

The Witchfinders is not flat out terrible but it isn't exactly something that lodges in the memory afterwards either. It's just a ho-hum bland filler sort of episode where nothing much happens and there are no great moments that you remember afterwards. The Witchfinders really should have been much more fun than this. It's not completely terrible but, like far too many episodes in series eleven, ends up being rather forgettable in the end.

IT TAKES YOU AWAY (Director - Jamie Childs, Writer - Ed Hime)

In this episode, the Doctor and her companions land in modern day Norway and encounter an isolated cabin where a blind girl named Hanne (Ellie Wallwork) seems to have been abandoned by her father. She seems to be terrified and under siege from a mysterious creature. Upon investigation, the Doctor discovers a mirror with no reflection that turns out to be a portal to the Antizone - a buffer-space between universes.

There's more subpar Tennant/Smith leftovers at the start of this episode when the Doctor eats some dirt to deduce where they are and talks about a sheep revolution. It's not very funny. One of the irritating things about series eleven is the way the Doctor is constantly given unfunny lines which reference unseen adventures or incidents in her past. "Oh, a windmill. I love a windmill me. I used to live in one with Oscar Wilde. That was on Mars. I think I invented windmills." One thing we can say is that these unseen adventures always sound a lot more interesting than anything we DO see the Doctor do in series eleven! The adventures we do actually see the Doctor partaking in during series eleven are consistently boring and forgettable.

It Takes You Away got some modest hype in Doctor Who fandom prior to transmission. This was, some suggested, going to be the classic episode we've been waiting for in series eleven. All seasons of post 2005 Doctor Who, however patchy, have rewarded the patience of the viewer with some great stories. You know that you'll get something really good in the end even if you have to sit through a few filler episodes to get there. That's the routine with Doctor Who. Series eleven is the first season of 'Nu' Doctor Who where the viewer waits in vain for the elusive classic episode. It never arrives. The show never actually gets good. This is an entire season of Doctor Who stuck in first gear.

A cabin in the woods. A mystery. All ingredients for a good Doctor Who episode. Sadly, It Takes You Away is not the classic episode we were hoping for. The frustrating thing about It Takes You away though is that there is a good episode in here somewhere but it doesn't quite all come together. The mystery of the girl in the cabin and the unseen creature is all compelling enough at the start and although the mist shrouded Antizone feels like a vague rip-off of the Upside Down from Stranger Things, I actually enjoyed the parallel universe angle and these Antizone scenes because they give series eleven something it has sorely lacked - some craziness and eccentricity.

One of the big problems with series eleven is the fact that it has been so middle of the road. There is no ambition in this season and no big story arc. Chris Chibnall seems to have gone into this with no plan and no enthusiasm. He has simply produced ten mostly mediocre (and sometimes downright terrible) episodes of Doctor Who simply so that the BBC has something for their Autumn schedule. Chibnall's main goal seems to have been to want the series to be more accessible. There's nothing really wrong with (and even the biggest fans of Steven Moffat would admit that he sometimes disappeared up his own metaphorical black hole by trying to be clever - those seemingly neverending arcs, the River Song saga in particular, a sometimes wearing exercise in indulgence) but Chibnall's removal of the characteristics that make the Doctor the Doctor and his removal of the familiar villains has literally sucked the heart out of the show.

Everything that made Doctor Who interesting has been jettisoned under Chibnall in series eleven. What is left is a bland show that seems more geared to children than adult Doctor Who or general sci-fi fans. I would contend that even this was a failure. What child would be entertained by Demons of the Punjab or The Ghost Monument? I suspect they'd be bored out of their mind after ten minutes. Why would they be watching this dreary show? The best Doctor Who stories can be enjoyed by people of all ages. Chibnall has somehow made a show that is too slow and boring for children and too patronising and simplistic for adults.

Anyway, the fact that It Takes You Away is sort of bonkers at times is actually almost refreshing and charming after the constant diet of bland soup we have endured in series eleven so far. That's not to say that It Takes You Away is a great episode. It isn't. Like most of series eleven it is disappointing. However, this is the first episode in series eleven that is less than the sum of its parts. This could have been good. It had potential. Most of series eleven is not even less than the sum of its parts. Most of the episodes in series eleven have no parts. Series eleven is a glass of tap water. There is nothing there besides some fancy new cameras to make the locations look nice. It is empty and vacuous. It is boring.

The big reveal in It Takes You Away is the gang encountering Grace again. Only it's not the real Grace. This is the work of the Solitract - an entity who has created its own universe and wants companionship. Bradley Walsh continues to do the best work out of this cast (admittedly he doesn't have much competition) when Graham meets Grace again but must accept it is an illusion. Sharon D Clarke is rather wooden in her return as Grace and because series eleven has been so forgettable these scenes don't have the power that they should. We just aren't invested in these characters and even Bradley Walsh has endured some 'friendly fire' in that regard.

Walsh is doing good work in series eleven but he's in a terrible show with some atrocious actors. If he was in a good version of Doctor Who with a great actor as the Doctor then his arc would have more emotion and power. Bradley Walsh as Graham in series eleven is like a pleasant little side dish in an otherwise awful meal that gave you an upset stomach. He's the only good thing about what was a largely negative experience. Graham's ongoing attempts to get Ryan's approval and be called 'Grandad' are not helped by the fact that Ryan comes off as unlikable by being so snotty to Graham through series eleven. Ryan doesn't even deserve Graham's patience.

There are more terrible villains in this episode. Some killer moths. Kevin Eldon is rather wasted as a double-crossing alien villain. This episode has what has become an infamous moment in Doctor Who history. The Doctor saves the others but remains with the Solitract. The Doctor must then persuade the entity to release her. What's so strange about this you ask? Well, the Solitract takes on the form of a CGI frog with the voice of Grace for this scene. Is this the moment that Doctor Who has finally jumped the frog?

Well, I don't know. I sort of like the weirdness of this scene. You'll either love it or hate it.

What is most fascinating about this scene is that Jodie (who is obviously on set reacting to nothing) is alone at last with a Doctor-rish sort of moment. What could be more Doctor-rish than bargaining with a strange entity? You can visibly see her trying to work out how to play this scene. This is the moment where you can finally see Jodie desperately groping for her own unique take on the Doctor. She doesn't quite manage to get there in the end does at least show tiny flickers of promise. Although I would contend that, on the evidence of series eleven, there are many actors (both male and female) who could play this part better than Jodie, you can see in this scene that she's capable of more than this season is allowing her to do.

There's some major problems with the It Takes You Away script - the chief of which is the fact that Hanne's father has tricked her into believing there is a creature outside so that she doesn't go out and he go can through the portal and be with his late wife (who is obviously an illusion). This is child abuse and yet at the end of the episode the Doctor makes no attempt to punish him or say much at all. He's just left with his daughter. The same daughter he abandoned and tricked!

It Takes You Away is not a very good episode but it is a sort of likeable one in a strange way because it's one of the few stories in series eleven where they at least seem to be trying. The writer of this episode has come up an actual sci-fi concept! I know alternate reality stories are not exactly original but at the very least this episode has a science fiction sort of premise. If the last act had been better and a more talented actor was playing the Doctor then this could potentially have been a good little episode.

As as stands though, It Takes You Away has a lot of the negative baggage we've become accustomed to in series eleven. Wooden acting, sluggish direction, no sense that any money is actually spent on this show, and a general sense that we are watching a science fiction show made by people who don't know how to make a science fiction show. It seems to be beyond anyone working on series eleven to nail one of these stories and make a really good episode.

I suppose one would have to give the writers a big portion of blame for that but the direction, pacing, and acting in series eleven also leaves a lot to be desired. If you had to describe series eleven in two worlds you would simply say that it feels bland and uninspired. It's little wonder that the main cast often look bored in series eleven. It Takes You Away is flawed but interesting. This could have been a really good episode but somehow ends up as less than the sum of its parts.

THE BATTLE OF RANSKOOR AV KOLOS (Director - Jamie Childs, Writer - Chris Chibnall)

Set on the planet Ranskoor Av Kolos, the Doctor must stop the alien Stenza Tzim-Sha (Samuel Oatley) from using the powers of the psychic race the Ux to shrink the Earth in revenge for his previous defeat and exile thousands of years earlier. The heart sinks in this episode when you realise that the big surprise is the return of 'Tim Shaw' as the villain. Honestly, who cares? The Battle of Ranskoor Av Kolos would have been a passable (if mediocre) early or mid-season episode but as a series eleven finale it is very underwhelming.

They really pushed the boat out in this episode as far as the budget went. We get a quarry AND a warehouse. It's safe to say Tim Shaw (who seems to have wandered into the wrong show from an old Red Dwarf episode) is not the most formidable villain to grace Doctor Who. Ultimately, he is no match for a fiftysomething bus driver and his dyspraxia suffering grandson. The story in this episode riffs on The Pirate Planet and Logopolis. There's an anti-faith message (the religious aliens are depicted as idiots) in this story that feels rather smug and plenty of nonsense about neural blockers. There's an obvious joke that we could all with neural blockers to remove the memory of series eleven. The Battle of Ranskoor Av Kolos (battle? what battle? you won't get a battle in this episode!) is classic Chibnall in that the early premise goes absolutely nowhere.

If there is one thing we have learned about Chibnall in series eleven it is that he's is absolutely clueless when it comes to conjuring an ending to his scripts. They all just fizzle out in unsatisfying fashion. There's no peril either in this episode. The Earth is supposed to be in great danger from Tim Shaw but we see scant evidence of that. Fine actors like Mark Addy and Phyllis Logan are criminally wasted in underwritten supporting roles and the ultimate defeat of Tim Shaw is laughable.

There is something in this episode though that has been sorely lacking in series eleven and is sorely needed. Tension and drama between the main characters. It arrives here (at last) when Graham tells the Doctor he is going to kill Tim Shaw as revenge for the death of Grace and the Doctor warns him not to. And yet, even this welcome piece of tension never really goes anywhere. It might have been more interesting to have Graham disobey the Doctor. Graham decides not to kill Tim Shaw so puts him in a stasis chamber, presumably forever. This is actually worse than killing him and leaves an unpleasant taste in the mouth.

Jodie is still conspicuously 'acting' at times in The Battle of Ranskoor Av Kolos. She's bland and sort of annoying. The Battle of Ranskoor Av Kolos is the sort of thing that Capaldi would have elevated somewhat just by his presence. Jodie can't do that. Jodie's endless 'face scrunching' is really annoying by this late stage of series eleven. The dialogue in this finale is absolutely terrible. Chibnall continues his bizarre habit of having the Doctor constantly explain everything to the audience while precious little happens elsewhere in the way of action or spectacle.

It leads to a script full of lines this: "The Tardis is reporting that the planet's transmitting violent psychotropic waves throughout its atmosphere. The type of waves that mess with your brain, distort reality, change moods to the extreme. These are neural balancers. So long as you're wearing one, it should keep you immune to the waves. But you must keep it on at all times." And this: "This is one of the ships that sent a distress signal. Cryo-sleep chambers, long-range craft, weapons archive. Been in service for a long time, by the looks of things. But who sent the signal? Where's the crew?"

It is almost unbearable how boring Chris Chibnall's scripts are in series eleven. This is the finale and he displays no ambition whatsoever. He just presents your average bog standard dull Chris Chibnall story. Jodie continues to speak Chibnall's terrible lines as if she has cue cards all around the room. She gives them no meaning. Her acting adds nothing of interest to this part. The good news is that we get some TARDIS scenes in this episode. Sadly, it's hard for the cast to sell the awe and wonder of the TARDIS when the new interior set still looks like the Match of the Day studio. No wonder they had so few scenes in the TARDIS this season.

The TARDIS interior in series eleven looks ridiculous when the characters are all there. It's so small they have nowhere to stand. It just looks like a small empty room with a couple of crappy plastic props that are supposed to be crystals. Contrast this to the amazing TARDIS interiors that Tennant, Smith, and Capaldi had. Chibnall's lashings of technobabble makes the episode even more boring than it already is. The Doctor's masterplans are supposed to be great moments but in Chibnall's Who we can barely stay awake through them. In this episode there are robots who shoot each other when Ryan and Graham duck. Is this episode written for six year-olds? How does this stuff even get on the screen?

Chibnall makes the Doctor a complete idiot for most of these stories and then suddenly has her realise what is going on right at the end. He makes the Doctor constantly explain the plot as if the audience is stupid. One mistake (that we've already mentioned a billion times) in series eleven that The Battle of Ranskoor Av Kolos suffers from is the lack of an arc.

As the individual episodes were quite dull and there was no ongoing thread (with the promise and anticipation of it leading up to a big finale) through the season, there was really little to keep you watching. As a result, The Battle of Ranskoor Av Kolos must rank as the least anticipated finale since the show came back in 2005. The Battle of Ranskoor Av Kolos is basically the 'what the hell are we still doing here?' episode. Series eleven has largely been a complete waste of our time.

RESOLUTION (Director - Wayne Yip, Writer - Chris Chibnall)

In 9th century England, three tribes defeat a monstrous enemy. They break the body into three and place it in different parts of the world - just to be on the safe side. The last piece is discovered centuries later in modern day Sheffield by archaeologists. Well, to cut to the chase, the 'monster' is a Dalek. In squid form, the Dalek has secretly attached itself to the archaeologist Lin (Charlotte Ritchie) and now controls her. It seeks to reconstitute itself into its Dalek form and take over the world (or something like that). Needless to say the Doctor and her beloved fam will have to save the day.

Well, we finally get a familiar monster in the Chibnall era. They tried to be vague on the fact that Resolution would feature a Dalek and keep it secret but it seemed to become open knowledge that the most iconic of all Doctor Who villains would be returning before the episode was transmitted. Unusually for Doctor Who, this special was broadcast on New Year's Day rather than Christmas Day. That move might partially explain why the ratings were not very good. The other explanation would be that viewers had deserted Chibnall's Who in their droves by now.

Anyway, can the hapless Chris Chibnall redeem himself with a cracking Dalek story? No, not really but Resolution is at least an improvement on most of series eleven. Resolution has a bit more zip and energy than the tepid series eleven. The better pacing is presumably thanks to director David Yip. This is practically the only Chibnall era episode so far that actually seems to be trying to give you an entertaining ride. Most of series eleven felt like it was specifically designed to bore the audience to death.

Resolution is more watchable than most of series eleven but it is also subject to some of the many shortcomings we've grown accustomed to in any script by Chris Chibnall. Resolution's decent support casting and quicker pace is frequently negated by some blundering problems that we've already had our fill of in series eleven. One of the main problems here is Chibnall's hamfisted attempts at drama - which seem jarring and out of place in what is supposed to be a fun sci-fi show. Ryan's deadbeat dad (what does Chris Chibnall have against dads!) finally turns up and is played by Daniel Adegboyega.

Hands up who was greatly excited at the prospect of Ryan's dad turning up. No one I would suspect. We have to endure a seemingly endless scene where Ryan takes his dad to task in a cafe. It is suddenly like watching the dreariest episode of EastEnders ever made. Ryan's dad turns up out of the blue trying to sell a microwave oven to the cafe owner. This makes no sense. Is Ryan's dad a thief? Who on earth purchases second hand microwave ovens from complete strangers? They are as cheap as chips (and brand new!) online and in supermarkets. Does Chris Chibnall actually live in the real world?

Chibnall's script includes some baffling moments which were presumably his clumsy attempts at amping up the political correctness quotient of his script. At one point a character (who only features in one scene) announces he is gay about ten seconds into a conversation with a stranger. Is this not patronising? Do gay people all go around suddenly announcing their sexuality to complete strangers at the drop of a hat? Did Chibnall suddenly think the script was lacking a gay person? Answers on a postcard please.

Another perplexing moment arrives when the Doctor is told that UNIT doesn't exist anymore because of budget cuts.

What about Torchwood or the Shadow Proclamation? Captain Jack? Has Chris Chibnall ever watched Doctor Who? It is equally possible that Chibnall's deeply unfunny UNIT joke is a dig at Tory austerity. Well, ok, fair enough. It's still isn't very funny though. Even less funny is the scene where the Internet crashes and a family is forced to talk to each other on New Year's day. This is another Chibnall joke that lands with a thud. It would make some sort of sense if this was the usual Christmas Day episode but New Year's Day? Do families all stay together on New Year's Day? I've never been aware of January the 1st being a big family day in the way that Christmas Day is.

You might be thinking that the arrival of a Dalek will finally give Jodie Whittaker that big moment we've been waiting for. The moment where she finally shows some inner steel and charisma and magically becomes the Doctor. That moment never arrives. Faced with the Dalek she is quickly reduced (yet again) to gurning and pulling funny faces. "Get off this planet. This planet is protected by me and ma mates!" It's like being threatened by Su Pollard and a gaggle of infants. Plot holes in this episode include medieval soldiers defeating a Dalek, and Lin building a Dalek from some scrap metal in a barn. The A-Team have nothing on this woman. You thought the Doctor building a sonic out of spoons was far fetched? You haven't seen anything yet. What is the Doctor's plan in this episode? She seems to just point her sonic at everything as if it is a magic wand.

The pesky Dalek problem is ultimately solved by - drumroll - a microwave oven. How fortunate that Ryan's dad happens to drag a microwave oven around with him at all times. This is the Kryponite to defeat the Daleks. A microwave oven. Those Gallifreyans might have been advanced but they'd obviously never got around to developing microwave technology.
We can probably sleep soundly in our beds now with the

knowledge that Earth - festooned with microwave ovens as it is - will now never be at the mercy of the Daleks ever again. I look forward to the episode where the Cybermen are defeated by the Soda Stream that Ryan's dad has been unsuccessfully trying to sell to greasy spoons.

At one point in Resolution we think Ryan's dad is going to get sucked out of the TARDIS with Ryan. We feel absolutely nothing for these characters so the moment has no tension. If Jodi's Doctor was going to be sucked out of the TARDIS you probably wouldn't care. By this late stage of series eleven (Resolution is a 'special' but it's more or less a part of series eleven), Chris Chibnall seems to have almost completely forgotten that he created a character called Yaz. You have to feel sorry for Mandip Gill. Yaz is basically reduced to standing in the background and asking a few questions now and again.

And yet, Charlotte Ritchie and Nikesh Patel are actually quite good as the archaeologists who stumble across this strange find in Sheffield. They actually have something between them that the main regular cast lacks - chemistry. On the evidence of this episode, Charlotte Ritchie would have been a much better companion that Tosin Cole or Mandip Gill.

For all of its faults though, Resolution is at least (the cafe scene aside) not boring. It has a bit of pace to it. It has some things happening. The scene where the Dalek takes out the soldiers is fun. That's the sort of thing we expect from Doctor Who. Resolution is not perfect but it's more entertaining than 95% of series eleven. It's the sort of thing that Chibnall should have done from the start.

SERIES 12

SPYFALL PART 1 (Director - Jamie Magnus Stone, Writer - Chris Chibnall)

The Doctor, Yaz, Graham, and Ryan are called into MI6 by C (Stephen Fry) to investigate some mysterious deaths. Their only lead is Daniel Barton (Lenny Henry), the CEO of a media company. The Doctor contacts Agent O (Sacha Dhawan), who was tasked with monitoring extra-terrestrial activities. C is killed by aliens, but the Doctor and her companions escape. These pesky dimensional aliens are mysterious indeed and what exactly is Daniel Barton up to?

Happily, Spyfall Part 1 is a vast improvement on the dreck we were served up in series eleven. It seems that Chris Chibnall has taken stock and changed course. If series eleven was all about distancing itself from the classic monsters and villains of Doctor Who to create its own identity (an experiment which clearly failed), then series twelve feels a lot like Chibnall trying to throw some fan service our way to get the show back on track.

Series eleven felt a lot like a show that wanted to reach out to people who wouldn't usually watch Doctor Who. It was like a soft reboot that eschewed the lore of the show. You didn't need to know anything about Gallifrey or Time Lords or River Song or Cybermen to watch series eleven. People flocked to the show in their droves to experience the all new Doctor Who. The viewing figures were incredible. But then, once they realised that the 'all new' Doctor Who was absolutely tedious, they deserted the show in their millions - leaving just the die-hards and people who had tuned in at the end to wait for Call the Midwife. Anyway, Spyfall Part 1 is the best episode of Chris Chibnall's Doctor Who. It's actually really good.

What are the ingredients that make Spyfall so much better

than anything in series eleven? Well, for one thing it's well directed and shot. Even the TARDIS interior looks much better than it did in series eleven. They've improved the lighting, the console, and added some stairs. We at least get a sense now that the control room is merely the entrance to a much larger ship. The TARDIS interior was preposterously cramped and cheap looking in series eleven but it looks much better in this season. The moment where Sacha Dhawan's Agent O is given a look 'inside the box' is fantastic. His geeky enthusiasm is very touching and they deploy a nice trick where they sort of shoot the TARDIS interior from a distance to give it a bigger sense of scope. Segun Akinola's music here is appropriately magical and his Bond riffs throughout the episode are nicely done too. There's definitely a bit of magic in Spyfall Part 1 at times. The only time we experienced this in series eleven was when the TARDIS reappeared at the end of The Ghost Monument.

Generally, Spyfall Part 1 is very enjoyable because it gives you all the stuff you wanted in series eleven but didn't get. There's the start of an arc here, a massive twist, a returning classic villain, plenty of action, and decent aliens foes (a race known as the Kasaavin). The dimensional aliens who feature in this episode are genuinely unsettling because they are so strange and unfathomable. There are some good tense sequences too like the scenes where the aliens take out the agents in Australia.

The scene where the aliens briefly seem to have infiltrated the TARDIS is great too. At long last we feel a sense of genuine danger for the characters in Chibnall's Who. This was desperately missing in series eleven. During the RTD and Moffatt era you always got a sense that the Doctor was a dangerous person to go on a journey with. Sure it was fun and mostly ok to travel with the Doctor, but you never quite knew what was around the corner. You could easily end up as a converted Cyberman or trapped in another dimension. That quality was lost in the Chibnall era but it returns here because the alien foes seem formidable and dangerous.

There's a nice sense of scope in this episode too that works well. Chibnall's Who will try and deploy this 'globetrotting' style again in series twelve later on to less impressive effect but here it is executed with great style. The supporting cast in this episode is very good. Stephen Fry has a brief but enjoyable cameo as the head of MI6 and Lenny Henry is effective enough as the mysterious tech genius Daniel Barton. The real star though is Sacha Dhawan. The big reveal at the end of this episode is that Agent O is really the Master and the reveal is quite, well, masterful. "I did tell you to look out for the spymaster. Or should that be spy... MASTER."

The flip that Dhawan does from the nerdy and kind Agent O to a thoroughly evil and oleaginous Master is absolutely wonderful. Dhawan does not hold back or give us a subtle Master. He is completely bonkers and over the top. And you know what? I love it. This is exactly what Chris Chibnall's Doctor Who needed. Some energy and over the top charisma. Mad twists. Old villains. We just sat through an entire season of Doctor Who where literally NOTHING happened and it feels like Spyfall is a (very welcome) reaction to that.

You have to love the fact that The Master has his Tissue Compression Eliminator and kept the real Agent O in a matchbox! Some fans felt that it was a little too soon to bring the Master after Missy played such a big part in the last Capaldi season. We knew though that the Master would eventually come back to Doctor Who though didn't we? Why wait? I think Chibnall was right to go for broke and throw the Master straight back into the fray. It's what the show needed. You never really get an explanation for where this Master comes from in the line of Masters but it doesn't really matter in the end. The Master is back and he's as mad as a hatter. Do you really need much more than that?

Sacha Dhawan's energy and exuberance at the end of this episode is very enjoyable but would this manic Master work in larger doses? What if he had to carry an entire episode? Well, Chris Chibnall will put this to the test later on in season twelve so stay tuned. This is definitely the best of the Chris Chibnall scripts so far on Doctor Who and there are even some sly jokes. Stephen Fry's C assumes that Graham is the Doctor at first and he won't be the last person in series twelve to make this mistake. This even led to a conspiracy theory that Graham was really a Doctor who had lost his memory! I personally like to think that Chris Chibnall having people constantly mistake Graham for the Doctor in series twelve was a meta response to smart alec grumps like me who watched series eleven and said Graham felt more like the Doctor than Jodie!

What of Jodie and the fam in Spyfall? Well, Ryan and Yaz get a bit more to do here when they have a separate mission to interview Daniel Barton. These characters seem a little bit better in this episode than they were in season eleven and enjoy few nice comic moments. Bradley Walsh is still enjoyable enough as Graham - offering a very human counterpoint to all the derring do and escapism. You get the feeling that Graham would prefer a comfy chair and a cup of tea to battling aliens. Graham is a good way to amusingly deflate the escapism with his down to earth nature. Series eleven was so dull that Graham had precious little escapism to play off but he works very well in the first of these Spyfall episodes that begin series twelve.

As for Jodie, well, there is no obvious quantum leap here in terms of her Doctor. She's still a middling actor who feels somewhat miscast and out of her depth. Jodie Whittaker, with respect, simply doesn't have the acting chops and natural charisma to carry this show in the way that actors like David Tennant and Matt Smith could. It's the reason why the really awful episodes in the Chibnall era feel all the more awful. If Steven Moffat produced a substandard story he at least had the saving grace of a Peter Capaldi or Matt Smith to mask some of the flaws in the writing with a commanding and charismatic lead performance. Jodie Whittaker, in contrast, simply sinks with the material.

What is nice though is the evening dress suit that Jodie wears with the bow-tie to infiltrate the big swanky casino function. A riff on the casino sequences in Bond films. It's amazing how a more Doctor-like costume makes Jodie seem so much more like the Doctor. I still think her costume should have been the dark 'hoodie' she wore in the short film they made to announce her as the Doctor. The 'snap' scene though when the Doctor gambles in the casino does rather illustrate Chris Chibnall's tin ear for humour. It is one of the big weaknesses of this showrunner. Russell T Davies and Moffat could make their Doctor Who scripts funny. Chibnall struggles with this aspect of Doctor Who and it really shows.

Yes, the motorcycle sequence is a bit too cartoonish and silly for its own good but we forgive Spyfall a few contrivances. What's great about Spyfall Part 1 is that it feels like they really pushed the boat out. The money is there on the screen with the locations and special effects. The big plane sequence at the end is terrific and very tense. It's fantastic to see the Doctor and these companions in real danger - something that was completely missing from series eleven. The Doctor is zapped out of the plane to who knows where - leaving Ryan, Yaz, and Graham trapped on an aircraft about to blow up. The Master, before he escapes, teases the Doctor with the cryptic line - "Everything that you think you know... is a lie." This is great because it's a hook to make us keep watching. It's a cliffhanger. Spyfall Part 1 is exactly what we wanted when we tuned into the start of series eleven but didn't get. It's fast, well made, has an interesting story, some good horror sequences, plenty of sci-fi, and rattles along in entertaining fashion.

You might reasonably ask where the Chris Chibnall who wrote and produced Spyfall was in series eleven. Spyfall is exactly what the first episode of series eleven needed to be like. If they'd come racing out of the gate this strongly in series eleven I think they might well have managed to hold onto more of the incredible audience who tuned in out of curiosity to watch Jodie's debut. I suspect that casual viewers were somewhat underwhelmed by The Woman who Fell to Earth and then simply bored by The Ghost Monument. One can easily see how casual audiences might have rapidly bailed out episode to episode. The double whammy of awfulness and tedium that arrived with Arachnids in the UK and The Tsuranga Conundrum must have been the final straw for many.

Spyfall, by contrast, shows us that Chris Chibnall at the top of his game is perfectly capable of writing good Doctor Who episodes and, happily, the direction and supporting cast are well up to speed too. All of the cast members get something to do, the story is mysterious in a way that provokes curiosity in the viewer, there are some good sci-fi horror elements, and it all builds to the fantastic twist. You have to love the Master's flying Australian bush house TARDIS at the end (a rather nice riff on The Wizard of Oz). That's a great moment when they all look out of the window and are utterly baffled. One thing we have to give Chris Chibnall credit for too is that he is a lot better at keeping secrets than Steven Moffat was. You can't imagine that the return of John Simm as the Master in the Capaldi era would have been completely spoiled in advance if Chibnall had been in charge. More than anything, Spyfall Part 1 is a welcome surprise. Spyfall Part 1 is a lot of fun.

SPYFALL PART 2 (Director - Lee Haven Jones, Writer - Chris Chibnall)

The Doctor is zapped into a strange dimension where she mets Ada Lovelace (Sylvie Briggs) and they are transported to 1834. The Doctor and Ada end up in Paris during World War 2 but are rescued by Noor Inayat Khan (Aurora Marion). The Master tracks her down and tells her that Gallifrey has been destroyed. The Doctor must somehow find a way to foil the masterplan that the Master, Barton, and the Kasaavin are somehow involved in.

Spyfall Part 2 doesn't feel as fresh as the opener of series twelve but it just about sticks the landing. It's a decent enough way to end the welcome return of the Doctor Who two-parter. Chibnall's habit of dumping too much exposition on the characters (not to mention the audience) is in evidence but, despite its flaws, Spyfall Part 2 is still a whole lot better than the stories we were forced to sit through in series eleven.

You might say that the historical figures Ada Lovelace (a pioneer in early computers) and Noor Inayat Khan (a spy) are shoehorned into this episode but I confess I didn't know much about these real life people and so it was interesting to see them in Doctor Who and learn more about who they were afterwards. One thing we should mention, and it's one of the reasons why these Spyfall openers work, is that we are not being spoon fed some preachy social message. We are, to our shock, actually having some fun! Spyfall Part 2 probably takes a little too long to get going but it has some lovely scenes and also gives Jodie's Doctor a few overdue and welcome moments of introspection and sadness.

The plane sequence cliffhanger is pretty good at the start of this episode. The Doctor has left a video message with instructions on how Graham, Ryan, and Yaz can survive. This scene is quite amusing. One thing that is welcome in Spyfall Part 2 is the way that the Doctor is separated from the companions. This is something that was much needed. Jodie needed more of a solo spotlight to cement her Doctor and she gets that here. At long last in this episode Jodie is starting to feel a little more like the Doctor. What helps of course is the fact that she has Sacha Dhawan to play against. Their scenes in Paris especially are very good. The Master tells the Doctor that Gallifrey was destroyed when they meet in the war torn city. The Doctor doesn't believe him but when she returns there at the end of the episode she finds only flaming ruins. She is distraught. At last we have some angst from this Doctor. It's one of the best moments for Jodie.

There's a nice scene too where The Master sends a message to the TARDIS and we see a hologram of him mocking the Doctor. He tells her that she is not who she thinks she is and that he destroyed Gallifrey in revenge for the lies they had been told. First things first. The TARDIS interior really does look much better in series twelve. They have clearly gone to the time and trouble of improving this set. As for Gallifrey, it looks as if this is the arc that will drive series twelve. You might argue that it's a bit soon to go back to Gallifrey (Hell Bent really doesn't seem that many episodes ago does it?) but, at this stage, we'll take it. We'll take Gallifrey over flying tea towels and The (Non) Battle of Ranskoor Av Kolos. It looks as if the 'Timeless Child' reference, which Chibnall floated a few times in series eleven, will play a big part in series twelve.

Sacha Dhawan hams it up somewhat when the Master appears in 1834, shrinking people left, right, and centre, but Chibnall's Who was so lacklustre and dull in series eleven that we desperately needed something like this. Chibnall had to go for broke at the start of series twelve to get us interested again and he does. This show needed the injection of energy that Sacha Dhawan supplies. Jodie is better in these Spyfall episodes but there are still some problems. We've probably accepted by now that's she never going to be great in this part. Notice the line where the Doctor says to the Master "What do you want?" after he's been manically shrinking people. Capaldi would have given this line so much subtext. So much weariness and defiance. Jodie literally just says the line as if she's reading it off her hand.

What doesn't work quite so well in this second part of Spyfall is Graham, Ryan, and Yaz. They go on the run from Barton and Chris Chibnall clearly struggles to find something for them to do. They have a nice scene where they hide out on a building site and Graham tries to rally them but their antics on the run soon become tiresome. The sequence where Graham dons 'laser shoes' is rather embarrassing and silly. There's so much stuff going on in these Spyfall episodes with the Doctor and the Master so maybe it was just unavoidable that there wouldn't be much room for the companions to thrive.

Lenny Henry's Barton makes a serviceable villain in the end but he does get a little lost as a character because there are so many other villains in this story. This is really a showcase for

Sacha Dhawan and although the Doctor zaps him to the alien dimension at the end we are fairly sure that we'll be seeing him again soon enough. There is no real explanation for which incarnation of the Master this is (in relation to Missy) but it doesn't really matter. We can simply speculate for ourselves. Villains in Doctor Who never really die. They can always return one day. What's nice about this version of the Master is that he's genuinely nasty and unhinged. The design of the scenes of the Doctor and the Master in war torn Paris are very well done with planes flying overhead and smoke billowing in the rubble.

Another overdue moment comes in this episode when the companions ask the Doctor about who she really is. Their apparent lack of curiosity in the Doctor always felt strange so this is an interesting moment. The Doctor looks pained though when Yaz asks if they can visit Gallifrey (which, of course, has just been destroyed). This is another good moment for Jodie. At last we have seen her Doctor display an inner life and a sense of a long and sometimes sad past. Chibnall has boldly thrown Gallifrey and the history of the Doctor back onto the screenwriting table. Will this gambit work? We will find out later in series twelve.

One other nice scene in Spyfall Part 2 comes when the Doctor must 'retrospectively' save Graham, Ryan, and Yaz on the plane at the end of the episode. She had completely forgotten about this so must come up with a plan - which we see her completing through a montage (a bit like the sequence where she made a sonic from spoons in The Woman who Fell to Earth). This is good fun. When the Doctor wipes the memories of her historical companions so they don't have knowledge of the future, this is quite touching.

The Doctor tells Ada that she doesn't need to know about the future. She'll work it out for herself. The human race will get there in the end. Chris Chibnall can often be hollow and pretentious when he tries to inject some heart into Doctor Who. One of his big weaknesses is to lean back into turgid 'straight' drama of the type that you might find in some ITV drama. In Spyfall Part 2 though he manages to inject some heart into the story without it feeling clunky or undeserved.

The scene in the TARDIS with the holographic Master is great because, in contrast to series eleven, the TARDIS now becomes almost like an extra character again just like it was in the RTD and Moffat years. Notice how the TARDIS interior seems to have turned blue to reflect the Doctor's mood. We get a lot more scenes in series twelve of the Doctor in the TARDIS and not only does this give the season more 'Who residue' than series eleven had, you can see that they did this because they have much more confidence in the TARDIS interior now. They've made it bigger, they light it much better, and it just looks more impressive. Happily, this means that Jodie can be seen in the TARDIS much more in series twelve and the TARDIS interior no longer seems so plastic, fake, and cramped. My own personal nitpick is that the console should still be bigger but I am happy to admit that they've improved the TARDIS interior considerably in series twelve.

Spyfall Part 2 takes a bit too long to get going at times and the escapades of Graham, Ryan, and Yaz on the run wear a bit thin in the end but - generally - this is a pretty solid end to the Spyfall run. We've established an arc, have the Master back, given Jodie some actual acting to do (as opposed to pulling funny faces and gurning), returned to Gallifrey, and seen a bit of charm and fun thrown back into the show. We are now (against all odds) actually optimistic about Chris Chibnall's Who again. We really want to see where it goes next. Spyfall Part 2 is not as strong as Part 1 of Spyfall but still one of the best Chibnall episodes of Doctor Who.

ORPHAN 55 (Director - Lee Haven Jones, Writer - Ed Hime)

Next up and the absolute nadir of the Jodie/Chibnall era we have Orphan 55 - the third episode of series twelve. In this episode, the Doctor, Ryan, Yaz and Graham are transported to Tranquility Spa, a luxury holiday resort world. However, the resort is threatened by monsters known as Dregs. The Spyfall episodes which opened series twelve indicated that Chris Chibnall had managed to refloat this sinking ship. We had our show back. We were excited again. This third episode takes us right back to square one. It is atrocious - easily as bad as anything in the last season. It is the worst episode of the entire Chris Chibnall era and, as anyone who sat through season eleven will tell you, that's really saying something! Where on earth do we even begin with this absolute trainwreck?

We begin to fear the worst from this episode early on when we meet the customer host of the luxury park - Hyph3n (Amy Booth-Steel). This host has some face paint that makes her look a six year-old child trying to be a cat or a squirrel at a fancy dress party. This is a character that would have been risible in the Sylvester McCoy era let alone 2020.

Ryan contracts a virus from a vending machine and while he recovers he meets Bella (Gia Ré). Tosin Cole, having shown signs of promise in Spyfall, is somehow worse than ever in these interminable flirting scenes. It often feels like Tosin can't quite remember how to do his Yorkshire accent and it somehow short circuits his ability to deliver convincing lines. Most depressing of all, Jodie is back to breathlessly explaining the plot to us every five minutes with a line delivery that sounds as if she's reading her dialogue from idiot boards. After all the good work they did in the Spyfall episodes, Orphan 55 somehow makes e Doctor annoying and bland again.

Orphan 55 had some production issues by all accounts and boy does it show. This episode feels unfinished and rushed. It is a complete fiasco from start to finish. There were apparently some problems with the monster suits and a lot of dialogue was recorded after the shoot and dubbed back into the episode. The shot of a 'Dreg' claw scraping against a wall is used so many times in this episode you genuinely wonder if they ran out of footage in the editing room. There are some obvious influences in this episode like the APC in James Cameron's Aliens and - of course - Planet of the Apes. The end of Orphan 55 is a complete rip-off of Planet of the Apes. Duh! We were on Earth all along and the Dregs are mutated humans. Get it? The 'dregs' of humanity. The episode called The Trap in the 1974 Planet of the Apes TV show also feels like an influence on Orphan 55.

You have to feel sorry for the guest stars in this episode. Julia Foster is awful as an elderly woman constantly shouting "Benni!" in search of her missing husband (Col Farrell). Inbetweeners star James Buckley is equally bad as a repairman with green hair. Laura Fraser as the dubious Kane (Alien reference?) is also forgettable. I actually felt sympathy for the cast (who are all abysmal) for having to appear in this tedious, amateurish, unwatchable nonsense. After the terrific supporting cast in Spyfall we hit rock bottom in Orphan 55 when it comes to the support players. None of these actors seem to have the faintest clue what they are even supposed to be doing in Orphan 55 and who can possibly blame them?

Tranquility Spa in this episode is not exactly Westworld. Sometimes it looks like South Africa and other times they could be literally anywhere. A local leisure centre or something. There are so few extras in this episode that the suspension of disbelief is completely negated. We see precious few guests on the screen to reflect a popular resort. When Graham settles down at the start to enjoy this 'paradise' location, he looks like he's at Pontins! The production design and direction is simply not good enough to sell the concept of the premise. We never really believe in Tranquility Spa as a place. Red Dwarf, a show which has no money at all up its sleeve, would have made Tranquility Spa more convincing than Orphan 55 ever manages to accomplish.

Tranquility Spa harbours a dark secret and there's much rushing around and shouting when chaos reigns. A lot of sound and fury that signifies nothing. You don't care about the (barely coherent) plot or any of these characters. When the characters take to an armoured vehicle on a dusty road they could be anywhere and you wonder why they didn't just save the money (and environment!) and film this in a quarry or on a beach in Wales. The music in Orphan 55 is literally an industrial hum in the background. It quickly becomes irritating in Orphan 55. Julia Foster shouting "Benni!" quickly becomes irritating in Orphan 55. Jodie as the Doctor quickly becomes irritating in Orphan 55. Entire scenes playing out in the dark quickly becomes irritating in Orphan 55.

James Buckley and his son having green hair quickly becomes irritating in Orphan 55. The squirrel woman quickly becomes irritating in Orphan 55. The complete lack of a plot or any coherence quickly becomes irritating in Orphan 55. The shot of the Dreg claw scraping the wall quickly becomes irritating in Orphan 55. The complete emptiness of this drivel quickly becomes irritating in Orphan 55. This is dour, incoherent, annoying, tedious. Orphan 55 is a complete waste of our time. I genuinely believe this episode must have done some damage to the ongoing ratings of series twelve. Can you picture people who might have been enticed back by the positive reception to Spyfall and then subsequently watched Orphan 55? Could you really blame them for bailing out again after this disaster?

Let's move to the much discussed ending. The Dregs are mutated humans who evolved after the Earth was ruined by our constant damage to the environment. "Look, I know what you're thinking, but it's one possible future," the Doctor tells the 'fam'. "It's one timeline. You want me to tell you that Earth's going to be okay? Cos I can't. In your time, humanity is busy arguing over the washing-up while the house burns down. Unless people face facts and change, catastrophe is coming. But it's not decided. You know that. The future is not fixed. It depends on billions of decisions, and actions, and people stepping up. Humans. I think you forget how powerful you are. Lives change worlds. People can save planets, or wreck them. That's the choice. Be the best of humanity. Or be the dregs of humanity."

This speech gives new meaning to the term 'on the nose'. I think we all managed to get the message of Orphan 55 without needing the Doctor to explain it to us at the end. It is this sort of thing that gives fuel to those annoying YouTube grifters forever moaning that Doctor Who is too 'woke' and preachy. Look, everyone agrees that pollution and environmental damage is bad. I do not eat meat. I do not own or drive a car. I let the garden grow wild for insects and birds. You can count on one hand the amount of times I've been on a plane in my life. I really do not need a patronising lecture on being 'green' from a wealthy Doctor Who writer who has probably been on an aeroplane more times in the last few months than I have in my entire life. And where did they film Orphan 55? South Africa! The week that Orphan 55 came out I put YouTube on and saw Jodie in New York being interviewed. That's all a lot of air miles isn't it for a cast and crew?

Just stop it Doctor Who. Stop lecturing us in a patronising way about things that we ALREADY know. We AGREE with you. You don't need to hammer us over the head with this obvious stuff. Lace your positive social and ecological messages into an entertaining and thought provoking sci-fi story. Don't produce 50 minutes of unwatchable drivel and then have Jodie come on at the end and say, "Well, idiots, just in case you MISSED the point, I'm now going to slowly explain it to you as if anyone watching this show is stupid." Orphan 55 is just the pits. Orphan 55 deserves to be in that landfill site where those Atari copies of the E.T game were dumped. This is, I think, the absolute worst episode of Doctor Who since the show came back in 2005. It makes Love & Monsters look like Wild Strawberries.

The worst thing about Orphan 55 is that it dissipates all of the optimism and hope generated by the Spyfall episodes. We are now depressed and gloomy about the show again (a state which many of us experienced on a regular basis during the long slog through season eleven). How can we go from Spyfall to Orphan 55? The drop in quality is mystifying.

Watching this episode we are reminded that when Doctor Who is bad in the Chibnall era it is bad in a way that almost defies belief. And that, sadly, applies to Orphan 55. This episode is so bad you can't actually believe it was produced and then broadcast. You genuinely wish it didn't exist.

NIKOLA TESLA'S NIGHT OF TERROR (Director - Nida Manzoor, Writer - Nina Metivier)

In 1903, the Doctor helps prevent Nikola Tesla (Goran Višnjić) from being kidnapped by the Skithra aliens. Well, thankfully, Nikola Tesla's Night of Terror is an improvement on Orphan 55. You wouldn't say this was a vintage episode but it's not bad for what it is. Not especially good but not bad. The best thing this episode has going for it is Goran Višnjić as Tesla. Višnjić is terrific here as the electrical engineer, inventor, and pioneer and his anachronistic dark good looks make him perfect for this historical caper. This is another guest star who would clearly make a better Doctor than Jodie. When we see Goran Višnjić in the TARDIS you sort of wish he WAS the Doctor. To be fair to Jodie though she does manage to hold her own in her scenes with Višnjić. The beginning of this episode does illustrate an essential weakness of Chris Chibnall's Doctor Who - in that you often actually dread the arrival of Jodie and the 'fam' at the start of each new episode. That can't be right can it?

One thing that is nice though in this episode is that we see the 'fam' in some period clothes. It always felt odd in series eleven when they turned up in some historical time period wearing contemporary clothes. There's quite a good supporting cast in this one - for the most part. Robert Glenister's American accent is dodgy (and his character rather cartoonish) but he's a commanding presence nonetheless as a scheming Thomas Edison. There's a nice theme in Nikola Tesla's Night of Terror where Tesla and the Doctor bond because they have much in common. Both are outsiders, scientists, and inventors. Both are considered eccentric.

Tesla was Serbian and so sometimes felt as if it was more difficult for him to be accepted in America. Nikola Tesla's Night of Terror has an obvious subtext about the positive contribution that immigrants can make to a society and - happily - this theme is (for the most part) incorporated into the story in a fairly natural way. We don't feel as if we are being patronised or virtue signaled to death. Nikola Tesla's Night of Terror is an example of how you can have positive social messages in the show without treating the audience like complete idiots.

As far as the cast in Nikola Tesla's Night of Terror goes, the weak link is Anjli Mohindra - who was of course Rani Chandra in The Sarah Jane Adventures. Mohindra is the chief baddie here - Queen of the Skithra. This character is so similar to the Racnoss Empress from the David Tennant era that everyone presumed it would be the same alien. Anyway, the Queen of the Skithra just doesn't work in this episode. This panto villain is awful and the scenes featuring her feel silly and unconvincing. Watching these scenes one can understand why some Doctor Who fans often yearn for a pure historical that doesn't feature aliens.

It's always jarring too the way that the Queen of the Skithra has a humanoid body. It makes the 'monster' look too fake. The weakest parts of Nikola Tesla's Night of Terror come when aliens and special effects are deployed. Chibnall's Who sometimes feels slipshod and amateurish to me in a way that the Moffat era never did. That amateurish quality is in evidence here during a chase scene involving aliens in the street. The suspension of disbelief just isn't there. It never quite feels convincing as a setpiece.

The plot here is somewhat predictable. The Skithra deduce that Tesla (a man who wasn't really appreciated in his own time, which is one of the reasons the Doctor admires him - Tesla was a futurist) is the real genius of this age and want to kidnap him to help them scavenge through the universe. The Doctor and her companions naturally help to save the day.

Yes, it doesn't really make much sense for an advanced alien race to need an inventor from 1903 but you probably shouldn't be looking for airtight logic in an episode of a sci-fi show like Doctor Who.

The period details are not bad at all in Nikola Tesla's Night of Terror and one could imagine this as a decent romp in the RTD era. If one had a criticism of Nikola Tesla's Night of Terror it would be that this is never the most exciting of episodes. It is a bit dull in places and takes a nosedive when the Queen of the Skithra is introduced. The strong performance of Goran Višnjić does mitigate some of these flaws though - if not all of them. Nikola Tesla's Night of Terror feels a lot like a filler episode but that's not necessarily a criticism. This is not a massive episode on the scale of the Spyfall openers but it is relatively engaging in its best moments and the story is quite nice. As far as filler episodes of Doctor Who go, this is far from being the worst one.

You get the sense here that the writer Nina Metivier (a script editor in season eleven) is much more at home with the domestic Tesla scenes than she is with aliens and sci-fi. There's a nice, cosy period atmosphere developed here that is then gatecrashed by the Doctor and fam and all the nonsense with aliens. Thinking about it, with a more subtle threat and more of Tesla, this could have been a very good episode indeed. It's not bad but it never quite manages to really draw you in or become anything that lingers in the memory for very long afterwards.

It's nice to see Yaz paired up with Tesla in this episode in an attempt to give her more to do but these companions still feel undercooked all the same. There is just something about the core TARDIS team in the Chris Chibnall era that doesn't quite click. They never really gel together. If you look at something like Stranger Things, which has a large cast, it's masterful the way that the characters interact. In the third season season of Stranger Things there's a scene where the characters all meet up together in a mall after a tense encounter with baddies (where Eleven uses her powers to throw a car) and the way the camera sweeps around them as they all talk at once makes the scene feel completely natural.

Contrast this with Chibnall's Who when the Doctor and the fam are together. When the Doctor talks to them in the TARDIS they are frequently just standing in a line waiting for their turn to deliver a piece of dialogue. It doesn't feel natural the way they interact with one another. It feels wooden and staged. I'm not sure if that's the fault of the writer or the director but it's definitely something that could have been worked on and made much better.

There's some odd character details in this episode with the Doctor. She gives Graham a gun and seems happy to deploy a death ray. This feels inconsistent with the Doctor that lectured 'Not Trump' about guns in Arachnids in the UK. I suppose there is not absolute continuity when it comes to the Doctor. It does tend to lend credibility though to the view that the writers and Jodie have never really managed to get a firm grip on her Doctor.

The most familiar criticism of Jodie's Doctor is that she feels too human and that's still the case. You could believe that Matt Smith was an alien. You could believe that Tom Baker was an alien. You could believe that Peter Capaldi was an alien. Jodie still feels too normal to be convincing as the Doctor. You need an actor with more natural eccentricity. An actor who can be aloof, angry, funny, and seize a scene through the sheer force of their personality. Jodie has simply never been able to do this. She had a few good moments in the Spyfall episodes but moments like that have been rare indeed.

Nikola Tesla's Night of Terror is probably a slightly overrated episode in that, after Orphan 55, there was genuine relief was it wasn't completely terrible for the second week in a row. In comparison to Orphan 55, Nikola Tesla's Night of Terror probably seemed a little bit better than it actually was. This is one of those run of the mill Doctor Who episodes where you find your attention wandering from time to time but, on the whole, it's ok. It's average but (thankfully) not dreadful like the previous week. You probably wouldn't go out of your way to watch Nikola Tesla's Night of Terror again but it's not bad for what it is and Goran Višnjić is terrific casting as Tesla.

FUGITIVE OF THE JUDOON (Director - Nida Manzoor, Writer - Vinay Patel and Chris Chibnall)

The Judoon (intergalactic police) arrive in Gloucester looking for a fugitive. The Doctor decides to intervene to see what they are doing. The mystery seems to revolve around a seemingly ordinary couple named Lee and Ruth Clayton (played by Neil Stuke and Jo Martin respectively). This puzzling situation is further complicated by the mysterious Gat (Ritu Arya), who seems to be an alien contractor.

Fugitive of the Judoon was the most bonkers episode of Chibnall's Who to date at the time and, generally, that's a good thing. We were told before transmission that this was a big episode with many surprises and it certainly is. This feels more like a finale than a bog standard mid-season episode and that was probably needed after the awful Orphan 55 and the decent but still largely forgettable Nikola Tesla's Night of Terror. Fugitive of the Judoon feels a lot like a RTD episode in its early scenes.

The Judoon are brought back into the show well enough (the design of their suits and ship is well up to par) and it is of course fun to see some previous characters from another era returning. Chibnall deliberately eschewed this type of thing in series eleven and it didn't really work in the end. It just feels much more like Doctor Who when characters and villains from the past return - as you long as you don't overdo it. Obviously, if you have the Daleks in every other episode you'll get sick to death of them but you can bring them and other classic Who characters back now and again.

We get a lot of focus on a woman named Ruth early on in Fugitive of the Judoon. Ruth is a tour guide who struggles to attract customers. We like Ruth although we are suspicious of her husband Lee and wonder if this is who the Judoon are after. This though will turn out to be misdirection. The proverbial red herring. One thing that doesn't work very well in the early scenes is Michael Begley as 'All Ears' Allan, a man who works as the bakery/coffee shop and seems to have taken a shine to Ruth. Allan is another reminder that humour is not the forte of Chibnall's Who. This comic relief character could easily have been jettisoned from the episode without losing anything.

We soon have the first big twist of the episode when Graham is separated from the group. He is zapped off to a strange ship and hears a voice talking to him that he doesn't recognise. We recognise the voice though. It's none other than Captain Jack Harkness! Jack appears and promptly kisses Graham - who he presumes is the Doctor. "You missed me right?" says Jack. Yes, we did. Ten years was far too long for Jack to be be missing from Doctor Who and it's great to see him again.

Much credit to Chibnall for keeping Jack's return a big secret. John Barrowman slips back into the part of Jack as if he's never been away and supplies the sort of fun and charisma that the regular cast of Chibnall's Who patently lack. Sadly though, we only see Jack with Graham on the ship in a few scenes and then he leaves. Jack tells Graham that the Doctor must be warned about the 'Lone Cyberman' and the universe could be at stake. Chibnall has clearly learned his lesson from series eleven. We've now had in series twelve the destruction of Gallifrey, the mention again of the Timeless Child, and now we've got cryptic warnings about a Lone Cyberman.

These are hooks that make us anticipate the rest of the season. Chibnall is seeding some interesting elements in season twelve that have us curious. This is exactly what season eleven lacked. If you make a season of stand alone Doctor Who episodes with no arc and those stand alone episodes are not very good then people have absolutely no good reason to tune back in again the following week. Series twelve is at least learning from some of the mistakes of series eleven.

As if the return of Captain Jack wasn't enough, we get another huge twist in this episode when Ruth seems to experience repressed memories (that seem to turn her into an instant ninja who can fight like Bruce Lee - I'm not sure this sort thing is at home in Doctor Who) that compels her and the Doctor to take a road trip to a light house. Ruth finds an alarm box and opens it - whereupon she is bathed in energy. Outside, the Doctor finds a buried TARDIS. Ruth now has her memories back. She knows who she is. She's the Doctor. This is a really big twist and one that Chibnall has never really explained.

First thoughts were that Ruth was a Doctor from an alternate universe but Chibnall debunked this theory and insisted that Ruth is a real Doctor. Ruth's TARDIS being a police box is a strange detail that is never explained either. Now, we've had, as any fan knows, hints before that there might have been Doctors before Hartnell but actually going down this path is controversial because not all fans like the history of the show being tinkered with. Some fans get very grouchy indeed if you do anything to suggest Hartnell wasn't the first Doctor.

Jo Martin won much praise for her portrayal of the Doctor and many argued that she displayed some the qualities that Jodie lacked (like gravitas and presence) and would have made a better first female Doctor. While I agree that Jodie remained frustratingly lightweight as the Doctor, I can't quite support the theory that Jo Martin is a great revelation in the part. There's nothing at all Doctor-like about Jo Martin and she's not exactly the most charismatic of actors. Compared to John Hurt (who was also a sort of surprise 'guest' Doctor), Jo Martin is a rather forgettable Doctor.

On the evidence of Jodie and Jo Martin you'd have to say that Chris Chibnall is not exactly a genius when it comes to casting Doctors. There are literally dozens of female actors in Britain who would make a better Doctor than either Jodie or Jo Martin. One thing I did find though, and it was a surprising sensation, was that when Ruth is revealed as a Doctor (from where though in the timeline we have no clue), I suddenly felt slightly protective of Jodie. Perhaps it was familiarity more than anything. Maybe I was just more used to Jodie's Doctor by this point. Not to knock Jo Martin, who is very good as 'Ruth' early on in the episode, I just didn't really agree with the consensus that she was amazing as the Doctor. That's a nice touch by the way that we get to see Ruth's very 'classic' TARDIS interior.

Fugitive of the Judoon is pretty good on the whole. It has that vague 'wonkiness' that most Chibnall era episodes have with some forced unfunny comedy and Ritu Arya as the mysterious Gat (who is revealed to be Gallifreyan) is a bit of a liability but - generally - this is an entertaining episode of Doctor Who. Things are happening, there are twists, it's competently directed, old villains and beloved characters return. The Captain Jack reveal is nicely done with a great soar of heroic music.

Fugitive of the Judoon is everything that series eleven wasn't. There is more stuff for those YouTube reactors to react to in Fugitive of the Judoon than the WHOLE of series eleven. Fugitive of the Judoon is confusing at times but you certainly won't be bored watching this. I think the key message that Chris Chibnall seems to have taken onboard is that people seemed to find series eleven boring. There was nothing in series eleven to really grab people or make them tune in again. It became a chore to sit through very quickly.

Once the novelty of a female Doctor had worn off (which happened as early as The Ghost Monument for me), the show felt hollow and lackadaisical. It felt too sedate and bland. Too smug and pleased with itself. Chibnall, in series twelve, has reacted to that. These early episodes in series twelve have more shocks, surprises, and twists than the whole of series eleven. It's a shame really that the unbelievably bad Orphan 55 disrupts the otherwise positive vibrations generated by the first block of episodes in series twelve. Fugitive of the Judoon doesn't always make sense but it has plenty of big surprises and is for the most part very entertaining.

PRAXEUS (Director - Jamie Magnus Stone, Writer - Pete McTighe and Chris Chibnall)

The Doctor and her companions investigate a bacterium that covers human bodies in a crystalline substance before disintegrating them. After the intrigue and surprises of Fugitive of the Judoon, series twelve now takes an unfortunate dip in quality. Praxeus is ultimately much ado about nothing. It begins in bizarre fashion with a couple of backpackers deciding to camp on a rubbish dump (as you do!) and encountering Ryan. The 'fam' have split up to investigate some strange events around the world. The 'globetrotting' nature of this episode is mildly interesting at first but your attention quickly starts to sag as Praxeus takes its own good time to go nowhere in particular.

Series twelve thus far has shown definite signs of improvement but Praxeus is very much in the vein of series eleven. Talky, a dull plot, uninteresting characters, and an obvious 'message' that you would hardly call subtle. The plot revolves around plastic waste in the Indian Ocean - which aliens have been drawn to looking for an antidote to the bacterium. Look, I said Praxeus had a plot but I didn't say it made much sense. This is another episode where we are lectured about ecological and environmental matters by a group of people who, carbon footprint be damned, flew all the way to South Africa to film this.

Do we really need Doctor Who to lecture us about plastic waste? I think we can all agree that plastic waste is bad. We probably don't need Chris Chibnall to remind us of this. It's not as if Doctor Who fans were all manically throwing plastic bags into the sea in their spare time and then suddenly realised the error of their ways after watching Praxeus. This heavy-handed preaching probably wouldn't matter at all if Praxeus was a great episode but it's pretty mediocre fare and so we sort of resent being patronised all the more.

Yet again in the Chibnall era we have been forced to sit through an absolute snoozer just to get to a patronising 'message' at the end. We thought we'd seen the back of this version of Chibnall's Who but Praxeus is an unwelcome journey back in time to the self-satisfied sleep inducing series eleven. There were a certain amount of complaints that Chibnall's version of Doctor Who was too political. Too preachy if you like. Some felt that the 'messages' had become more important than the stories. We should start by saying that Doctor Who has never been what you would call apolitical. There have always been subtexts and 'messages' in Doctor Who.

The Doctor (in his/her many incarnations) has always battled prejudice and intolerance. The Doctor always stands against oppression and the worst aspects of humanity (even if expressed through fictional alien races). The Doctor is a positive character with a positive message. Be kind and tolerant. Stand up against oppression in all of its forms. Don't be afraid to be different. There have been political subtexts in Doctor Who stories many times in the past. Look at the Daleks - the Doctor's mortal enemy. They clearly represent fascism.

There is nothing wrong with Chibnall wanting to have positive 'messages' in Doctor Who that reflect his thoughts on society. The mistake Chibnall made with the latter was to do this in a clunky and obvious way. Rather than dress up these messages in an entertaining fantasy story (in the manner that the always socially and politically conscious Rod Serling often did so brilliantly in The Twilight Zone), Chibnall makes it feel as if he is only making Doctor Who so that he can broadcast how liberal and enlightened he is.

Chibnall's stories are often threadbare and dull but suffused with bizarre moments like the random character announcing he is gay to a complete stranger within ten seconds of meeting them in Resolution. It makes the show feel self-satisfied and patronising. Chibnall's Doctor Who too often feels like the patronising product of a bunch of humourless middle-class writers sitting around a table trying to out PC one another. Make the stories great first and then lace in the message. Don't have an obvious patronising message in a dull story. That's the worst of all worlds.

Some might argue that Doctor Who returned to its roots as an educational show for children under Chibnall. I would argue that - if this was the intention - Chibnall didn't do a very good job. You don't actually learn that much about witch trials in The Witchfinders. You don't come away from Demons of the Punjab with a tremendously nuanced or deep knowledge of the partition of India. As for Rosa, I imagine that most children would be bored to tears by that episode. If you wanted to learn more about Rosa Parks you'd be better off reading a book or watching a documentary.

There was speculation that Praxeus was going to be a Sea Devils episode but that obviously didn't transpire in the end. The supporting characters in this episode are ex-police officer Jake (Warren Brown), who is compelled to track down his husband - astronaut Adam (Matthew McNulty). Adam is infected in a Hong Kong lab. There is also blogger Gabriela (Joana Borja) and medical researcher Suki (Molly Harris). One of these characters is not who they seem to be (which comes as no surprise) and all of them are rather dull. Praxeus is not one of those episodes where the supporting cast outshine the regular actors. You won't remember any of the characters in Praxeus for very long after you've watched the episode.

There's a lot of science gobbleygook as the Doctor searches for a cure (Jodie is back in babbling primary school teacher series eleven mode here and becomes especially irritating LONG before episode is over) and some attempted horror flourishes where birds turn violent. The scenes involving the birds are very poor indeed (the special effects are a little on the dodgy side in Praxeus at times) and Praxeus is generally one of those episodes where you spend a lot of time absorbing yourself with who the specific characters are and what the actual plot is and then realise at some early juncture that this is a terrible episode and so it's all been a waste of time and effort anyway.

This episode has some strange plot holes like the fact that Doctor spends an awful lot of time in a lab when surely she would be better off in the TARDIS? It feels as if Chibnall tries to justify the existence of Yaz in this episode by splitting up the team and having Yaz go off on a solo mission through a portal. While one can appreciate the attempt to remind us that Yaz is in this show (you really couldn't blame us for forgetting that fact from time to time), it does make Yaz appear a bit foolhardy and stupid and it does make it look like the Doctor doesn't take her duty of care very seriously. Out of the Doctors we've had since 2005, Jodie feels the one most likely to get one of the companions killed by not paying attention or making a stupid decision.

Yaz, despite the efforts of Chibnall, just isn't a very interesting character. We still feel like we barely know her. She has no real personality. It is truly bizarre. Yaz is just sort of there. We genuinely have no idea who she is or what her character traits are. Moffat, by way of comparison, had Bill Potts pretty much nailed down and established inside one episode. The end of this episode is especially stupid as Jake makes a sacrifice by piloting the alien to safety (it has an antidote which will explode in the atmosphere) but is then saved by the Doctor - who warps the TARDIS around the ship.

This effectively renders the sacrifice of Jake pointless. The scene was stupid enough to start with. It's hard to suspend disbelief when police officers can suddenly fly alien ships at the drop of a hat. Praxeus is just one of those Chibnall era episodes that doesn't click. Despite the effort it never feels like we ever get out of second gear. We are never engaged by what is happening and we don't really care about any of these characters.

A major problem with Praxeus too is that it more or less ignores Fugitive of the Judoon. We've just had Captain Jack and a mysterious new Doctor we knew nothing about but that's all forgotten for now. Praxeus is just business as usual. Nothing from last week plays a major role here. The presence of John Barrowman last week also (unavoidably you might say) reminds us of how dull the main cast is in the Chibnall era. The supporting players in Praxeus are pretty awful. Series twelve has been good when it comes to casting so far. We've had Sacha Dhawan, Goran Višnjić, Stephen Fry, Lenny Henry. Praxeus has no one like this though to lift the material.

One other thing about Praxeus that is sub-par is the music by Segun Akinola. Akinola can, in his best moments, provide heartwarming heroic cues for Doctor Who. However, far too often his scores become driving industrial sounding generic beats. Akinola is at his absolute worst in Praxeus. He is literally just telephoning in scores like this. It is in episodes like Praxeus and Orphan 55 that you appreciate all the more the work that Murray Gold (who, admittedly, is not everyone's cup of tea) did during his tenure on Doctor Who as the composer.

Praxeus is dispiritingly mediocre on the whole with some of the worst acting you are ever likely to encounter in a mainstream television show. This feels a lot like an episode where they wanted to be topical and environmental but couldn't manage to come up with a story that justified the theme. The worst thing about Praxeus is that it gives you unwelcome series eleven flashbacks. There's far too much standing around talking, Jodie is annoying again as she constantly babbles to herself and orders people around like a primary school teacher on a field trip, and then the patronising green message about plastics.

Praxeus is an episode that seems to have learned absolutely

nothing from series eleven. It is puzzling really because it was directed by Spyfall's Jamie Magnus Stone in the same shooting block. You would have expected this episode to be much better but then a director can only do so much with a convoluted and ultimately empty script. As far as the rest of the cast goes, Tosin Cole feels more wooden than usual although Bradley Walsh has his moments as Graham. Walsh is easily the best thing about the regular cast but, alas, even he can't save episodes like Praxeus on his own. This is a very mediocre episode with poor performances from the cast. The 'message' about plastic waste is delivered with all the subtlety of Captain Planet and the Planeteers.

CAN YOU HEAR ME? (Director - Emma Sullivan, Writer - Charlene James and Chris Chibnall)

From ancient Syria to Sheffield, the Doctor (Jodie Whittaker) and her companions are stalked by a strange being who forces them to confront their worst nightmares. Can You Hear Me? has some potential but the end result is, unfortunately, simply more series eleven flashbacks in the end. This episode ends with the BBC giving you a mental health helpline number to ring if you've been affected by the themes of the story!

We can all agree that mental health is an important issue but I also think we can probably agree too that we watch things like Doctor Who to escape from the real world and our problems. I must have missed the announcement that Chris Chibnall had been appointed as the nation's social worker and had decided to impart his great wisdom and healing through the medium of Doctor Who. Can You Hear Me? is the return of that clunky, pretentious, dour Chibnall from series eleven. The one who takes himself far too seriously.

The episode begins, after a period prologue in Aleppo, with the companions experiencing nightmares. Ryan witnesses a strange man detach his fingers and place them in the ears of his friend Tibo (Buom Tihngang). It's hard to dredge up much feeling for Tibo because we've barely met him in Doctor Who and just have to trust the writers that he's a great friend of Ryan. The 'floaty fingers' stuff is a bit creepy at first but quickly overplayed. By the end of this episode you'll be sick to death of the 'creepy floating fingers' palava. Generally though, the concept of the characters experiencing strange connected nightmares, while hardly original, is mildly interesting.

The episode starts to sag when the Doctor arrives in Aleppo, Syria, in 1380 to rescue a woman named Tahira (Aruhan Galieva). Jodie is babbling away to herself and quickly starts to grate. It would be awfully nice to see a quiet, calm, calculating Doctor for a change. The Doctor confers with Graham, Yaz, and Ryan and deduces that the TARDIS can find the source of Graham's vision. This turns out to be a spacecraft where someone seems to be a prisoner of a futuristic quantum fluctuation lock. This sort of stuff should be a slam dunk for Doctor Who. Moffat could have spun a very good episode from this but, despite the potential of the story, Can You Hear Me? manages to bungle most of the promise inherent in this concept.

The Doctor and the companions soon meet the big villain - the immortal Zellin (Ian Gelder), who is some sort of God. Gelder is perfectly fine in this part but does unavoidably (again) illustrate the lack of heft and gravitas that Jodie has in the main role. Jodie's Doctor just never seems very clever or formidable during big confrontation scenes. The Doctor is made to look rather foolish in this episode when she releases the prisoner - who turns out to be Rakaya (Clare-Hope Ashitey), an ally of Zellin. This diabolical duo plan to feed off nightmares on Earth but they are, of course, eventually defeated by the Doctor.

And what was the fiendishly brilliant masterplan that the Doctor used to defeat these Gods? Well, that's a very good question. I wish I had a satisfactory answer. The Doctor defeats the villains by luring them to Aleppo and waving her sonic screwdriver at them. That's it. This resolution is so out of the blue and underwhelming I genuinely wondered for a moment if I had missed part of the episode or if there was a scene missing. It is the laziest sort of ending imaginable.

The sci-fi stuff in Can You Hear Me?, like the spacecraft out in the great void, should be the foundation of a much better episode than we get here. The Doctor battling a God like villain should definitely be more fun and epic. Can You Hear Me? is just sort of bland and underwhelming in the end though. It feels like we are back in series eleven. It's a shame really because the neon spacecraft interior is quite good fun and you'd think that an episode concerning villains who feed off nightmares would be decent material for a scary and intriguing episode of Doctor Who.

It's all so tepid though. It feels flat and the main cast can never seem to inject much life into anything when they get a very average script. David Tennant and Catherine Tate would have made Can You Hear Me? 25% better merely by their presence. Capaldi would have made this infinitely more watchable. Jodie and the fam though sink down to average material rather than elevate it through acting savvy and charisma.

The villains are defeated but we aren't quite finished yet. Can You Hear Me? now festoons its ending with some signature Chris Chibnall attempts at drama. Yaz tracks down a police officer to thank her for the words of comfort she gave Yaz years ago when Yaz was depressed. And then we have the Doctor awkwardly snubbing Graham when he attempts to talk about his cancer. The scenes with Yaz and the police officer feel out of place. This doesn't feel like Doctor Who. It feels like Clocking Off or Holby City. We don't really care about Yaz because she's just a blank on the fringes of the show. Amy, Clara, Bill, Rose, Donna. These companions had character. They were (in whatever order you ranked them) big characters in the TARDIS. You knew they were there. Yaz is like the invisible woman in comparison. The blame for this must squarely lie with Chris Chibnall.

In the same way that giving Yaz a dramatic solo moment doesn't work because Yaz is so uncharismatic and vague, the return (again) of Grace in Graham's dream/nightmare sequences also feels hollow. While it is true the people seemed to like Sharon D. Clarke, the fact is that we met Grace for one single solitary episode before she was killed off. We barely knew her! It feels like ludicrously misplaced optimism to keep leaning back into the Grace character for a Graham tearjerker.

Finally, we come to the scene where Graham talks to the Doctor about his cancer and she gets all embarrassed and walks off. This scene drew some criticism and the BBC even recieved complaints. The point of the scene is that people find it difficult to talk about mental health and personal problems. That's clearly what the writers were trying to say. The problem is though that it made the Doctor seem as if she didn't care. Why doesn't she just take Graham to the future when they have a cure for cancer?

The Graham/Doctor scene is also inconsistent too. Do you remember the scene at Grace's funeral in The Woman Who Fell to Earth when the Doctor asks Ryan if his dad has arrived? In that scene, Jodie's Doctor is tender, understanding, and not socially awkward or afraid of listening to personal problems at all. They did the socially awkward Doctor thing with Peter Capaldi at first and the early Capaldi Doctor would definitely be all at sea trying to have a heart to heart about cancer. But Jodie's Doctor hasn't been like at all.

You'd think Jodie's Doctor, as written so far, would be the most approachable Doctor of all when it came to something like this. She's the Doctor who feels the most human. She's the Doctor who doesn't even feel like the Doctor! These misguided 'drama' moments at the end of Can You Hear Me? further compound the generally negative impression this episode has generated. While the sci-fi and horror concepts in Can You Hear Me? could have been fun and made for a good story, the end result here is disappointing to say the least. Can You Hear Me? is also pretty insufferable in the end.

THE HAUNTING OF VILLA DIODATI (Director - Emma Sullivan, Writer - Maxine Alderton)

The Doctor takes her companions to 1816 and to Villa Diodati on Lake Geneva to witness Mary Shelley (Lili Miller) gain the inspiration to write Frankenstein. However, they find the villa seemingly haunted, and Mary's future husband Percy (Lewis Rainer) has gone missing. A spectral figure appears and reveals itself as a Cyberman named Ashad (Patrick O'Kane) that is seeking the missing Cyberium, the collected knowledge of the Cybermen.

The Haunting of Villa Diodati is something of a return to form for series twelve after two disappointing episodes in a row. This episode is not perfect and takes a while to get going but it has bags of atmosphere and a decent supporting cast (who, as ever, outperform the regular cast). Jacob Collins-Levy is fun as a cocky Lord Byron and Lilli Miller is very good as Mary Shelley. The story here is sort of predictable in the end but it's enjoyable anyhow the way that a Cyberman becomes the inspiration for Frankenstein.

One salient factor in The Haunting of Villa Diodati is that it was written by Maxine Alderton - who was apparently employed as a script editor for series twelve. Although patchy in spots, the writing of series twelve has patently been better than series eleven and so Alderton must take a lot of the credit for that. On the evidence of The Haunting of Villa Diodati, Maxine Alderton would make a better lead writer for this show than Chris Chibnall.

The Haunting of Villa Diodati takes a while to get going and, as usual, the arrival of the Doctor and the 'fam' is grating as first but this episode begins to slowly draw us in and the constrictive nature of the spooky location works to the advantage of the story. One thing I really like here is the way that Graham seems to experience genuine supernatural events that are never really explained. It's a clever touch because we get a traditional ghost story that then morphs into a sci-fi yarn.

What I also like about this episode is that it seems a little dull at first but then gradually draws you in more and more by the sheer force of the atmosphere generated. Usually in the Chibnall era (especially of course in series eleven), an episode will start ok and then quickly lose your interest. The Haunting of Villa Diodati is the complete opposite.

The Haunting of Villa Diodati allows series twelve to finally pick up an arc again when we finally meet the 'Lone Cyberman' that Captain Jack warned Graham about. The Lone Cyberman character walks a very fine line here between being scary and being a silly Red Dwarf villain. Patrick O'Kane has a pretty thankless task here but he does his best. This (half-converted) character looks more human than Cybermen we've seen before so is something vaguely new I suppose.

The arrival of this character does give the episode a twist and fresh impetus. The ghost story we were getting was fine but it's fun all the same to suddenly get thrown back into a sci-fi story and pick up the thread from a few episodes back. The last third of this story serves as a good way to set up the two-parter to come. Thankfully, it appears that Chibnall is going to make the finale of series twelve a much bigger deal than the finale of series eleven was. We'll have to see shortly if he managed to make it good but at least he seems to be trying harder to make Doctor Who interesting again. Series eleven didn't really have a finale. We just got the return of Tim Shaw in a dull, forgettable episode.

What of the regulars in The Haunting of Villa Diodati? Well, after two weak performances in a row, Jodie is a bit better here. She does seem to raise her game somewhat. Tosin and Mandip are still wallpaper though. Tosin Cole actually seems bored in large parts of series twelve. I know it's hard to tell at times because Ryan is not the most demonstrative of characters but Tosin does definitely have at times the air of a man who wouldn't mind a change of scenery and a new character to play. Yaz is still undefined in series twelve despite some effort to give her a few solo moments. We've made this point before, but you can't really blame Tosin and Mandip. They are playing what they are given by the writer. If these characters seem dull and forgettable then that's the fault of Chris Chibnall. RTD and Moffat could fashion a memorable new character in the space of an episode but Chibnall clearly can't do that.

Graham does at least have some good moments in this episode. The easygoing and very human Graham remains by far the best companion although you can't help thinking that this is down to the likeable and amusing performance of Bradley Walsh rather than Chris Chibnall. It shows how important casting is. A great cast can lift average material. It's one of the reasons why Jodie makes for a very forgettable Doctor. She just isn't commanding or charismatic in the way that the Doctor should be (although I have heard that Jodie has displayed these qualities in her stage work).

A much stronger and more charismatic lead actor would have masked some of the flaws in Chibnall's writing and made the show feel better than it was. This is why Moffat cast Peter Capaldi as the Doctor. He wanted a strong and serious actor at the heart of the show. The Doctor should always be the best available actor the producer could get their hands on at the time. This clearly wasn't the case with Jodie. Let's be completely honest, Jodie got this part because she knew Chris Chibnall from Broadchurch. British television is festooned with brilliant female actors. Are you seriously telling me that they couldn't have found someone better than Jodie Whittaker?

The Cyberium stuff in The Haunting of Villa Diodati feels a little on the vague side and the details about how the tiniest ripple can affect history is somewhat clunky (this is the sort of detail that can be pedantically unpicked as inconsistent but it's ok as long as you don't think about it for too long). "His thoughts, his words inspire and influence thousands for centuries. If he dies now, who knows what damage that will have on future history? Words matter! One death, one ripple, and history will change in a blink. The future will not be the world you know. The world you came from, the world you were created in won't exist, so neither will you. It's not just his life at stake. It's yours. You want to sacrifice yourself for this? You want me to sacrifice you? You want to call it? Do it now. All of you. Yeah. Cos sometimes this team structure isn't flat. It's mountainous, with me at the summit in the stratosphere, alone, left to choose. Save the poet, save the universe. Watch people burn now or tomorrow. Sometimes, even I can't win."

One can sense the hand of Chibnall in some later parts of the script. He must have had some input because the last part of this episode, as we noted, picks up the Cyberman plot suggested by Jack and also leads into the two-part finale. When the Doctor jokes to Ashad "Have you ever considered breath mints?" this sounds suspiciously like an unfunny Chris Chibnall attempt at humour. The Doctor saves Shelley and then gives the Cyberman what it wants - the Cyberium. In saving the present she might have endangered the future. This is all somewhat contrived but we can't complain because Chibnall is trying to give us exactly we missed in series eleven - high stakes. Everything might be at stake if the Doctor can't fix the future. Chibnall is going to go all RTD and give us a big two-part finale.

The Haunting of Villa Diodati is good on the whole. The ghost story elements are enjoyable, it's well directed, the supporting cast do their job, and there's even a cliffhanger of sorts. You might argue that it's a bit too soon to be bringing the Cybermen back again for another finale but it's an indication that Chibnall is leaning heavily into the back catalogue of Doctor Who villains after the underwhelming response to his 'fresh slate' series eleven approach. The Haunting of Villa Diodati is (mostly) good stuff and a considerable improvement over the previous two episodes.

Series twelve desperately needed a good episode after Praxeus and Can You Hear Me? and, by and large, The Haunting of Villa Diodati manages to deliver. You could argue that this is one of the most interesting episodes of the Chibnall era. One of the frequent complaints about series eleven was the fact that you couldn't imagine wanting to sit down and watch any of the episodes again. They were tedious enough the first time around. Series twelve is different though. We've actually had three or four episodes that you would be relatively happy to visit again. For that at least, Chibnall and his team deserve some credit. The Haunting of Villa Diodati is a bit wonky in places but enjoyably atmospheric all the same.

ASCENSION OF THE CYBERMEN (Director - Jamie Magnus Stone, Writer - Chris Chibnall)

The Doctor and her companions must face the consequence of the deadly Cyber-Wars, banding together with the last humans as they defend themselves from the Cybermen and search for a way out. We've reached the start of the big two-part finale of series twelve. Can Chris Chibnall redeem himself after the terrible (non) finale in series eleven? Ascension of the Cybermen is a passable enough bridge to the conclusion. This episode zips along at a fast pace and is always watchable, although when you think about it afterwards it does feel a bit hollow - even slightly forgettable.

Ascension of the Cybermen reminds me of the New Year special Resolution in terms of its pacing and tone. Both of these episodes pass the time (especially compared to series eleven) but they wash over you very quickly and don't stay in the memory for very long. You wouldn't have them at the Doctor Who top table by any stretch of the imagination. They are still some distance below something like, for example, World Enough and Time.

We begin Ascension of the Cybermen with the last outpost of humanity in the future. The Doctor and companions arrive and it's all rather Walking Dead (ravaged post-apocalyptic community devoid of life) and quite good fun. When we see a Cyber shuttle overhead the special effects are very good. There are a few problems with this opening to the episode though. The 'cyber drones' (basically flying Cyberman heads) are very silly and the Doctor is made to look completely ineffectual when her plan is foiled, people die, and the fam scatter and separate. Also, why did the Doctor park the TARDIS so far away from the scene of confrontation? Was this merely so the director could get a nice shot of the fam emerging on the top of a hill?

Chibnall throws a confusing subplot into Ascension of the Cybermen where we keep cutting to a period version of Ireland where an orphaned young man named Brendan (Evan McCabe) seems to be immortal and grows up to become a police officer. What on earth is going on? Is he a Time Lord? Captain Jack? We'll get an explanation (of sorts) in the finale but it doesn't quite justify the inclusion of this subplot. It's like we keep suddenly being thrown into an Irish version of Heartbeat. This subplot drags the pacing of Ascension of the Cybermen and feels too 'twee' and Sunday night potboiler drama (which is ironic I suppose given that Chibnall's Who is shown on Sunday nights!) for a big Doctor Who finale.

Graham and Yaz become separated from the others in this story and end up with a ragtag group of human survivors on an escape ship. Their optimism is in stark contrast to the survivors. This does at least though give Yaz a few scenes where she has more of a spotlight and Bradley Walsh (as ever) remains the most watchable performer of the main cast. Graham and Yaz end up with Yedlarmi (Alex Austin), Ravio (Julie Graham) and Bescot (Rhiannon Clements).

The actors playing the survivors do their best but these characters will probably not lodge in your memory for very long after Ascension of the Cybermen has ended. Chris Chibnall definitely struggles at times to sketch in memorable supporting characters. It's nice to get out into space though again in Ascension of the Cybermen. Chibnall's Who has definitely lacked a bit of space opera. We also get a genuine sense of danger for Graham and Yaz here. They are a long way from the Doctor with no apparent way of getting back.

However, they chance upon a Cybercarrier and that might just be a solution to their problems. As long as the Cybermen on the ship don't wake up though. Meanwhile, the Doctor, Ryan, and a survivor named Ethan (Matt Carver) end up searching for Ko Sharmus - a place that contains a portal where humans can travel to the other side of the universe and escape from the Cybermen. Ko Sharmus turns out to be a person (played by Ian McElhinney) rather than a place. The portal opens and reveals the ruined Gallifrey and the cliffhanger ends with the Master appearing through the portal and telling the Doctor that everything is about to change. We had a feeling he'd be back for the finale so no surprise here but we'll take it because Sacha Dhawan has more charisma in his little finger than the Doctor and companions combined.

Ascension of the Cybermen always feels slightly as if its ambitions outweigh its budget (we never actually see that many Cybermen and they remain the worst shots in the universe - they have wonkier aim than Stormtroopers!) when it comes to special effects and extras but it manages to wring some tension from Graham, Yaz, and the humans lurking around the ghostly Cybercarrier. It feels a bit like a RTD first-part finale - only without the wit and memorable characters.

My main problem with Ascension of the Cybermen is that while I was never bored I always felt somewhat unsatisfied. It never quite clicks into full gear and despite all the things that are happening and the various twists it feels slightly empty in the end. Ascension of the Cybermen is strange in the way that it zips along at a rapid rate but also feels like it is treading water and holding everything back for the final episode. Obviously, it IS holding back for the final episode but, all the same, it never quite falls in place and becomes a classic episode in its own right.

The character of Ashad still doesn't quite work for me in Ascension of the Cybermen. He's a very panto villain and maybe the Cybermen have been used too many times in recent years to muster much enthusiasm from the audience. It's like when Star Trek endlessly brought the Borg back. They just lost their novelty in the end. It's something slightly new to have a half-converted Cyberman but, all the same, maybe Cybermen were the classic villain that needed a slightly longer rest? It feels strange that in recent Doctor Who practically every finale has featured the Master and Cybermen!

Ian McElhinney is pretty good as Ko Sharmus at the end of this episode. He adds a bit of gravitas to Ascension of the Cybermen when he appears. What of Jodie in this episode? Well, it's nice to see the Doctor appear angry, stern, and worried at the start. Pretty soon though she's back to the perky, babbling Doctor that we've grown to know during the Chibnall era. With the best will in the world I don't think anyone can put Jodie in the gallery of great Doctors (at least not with a straight face) but she's had a bit more to play with in series twelve. Jodie is better than she was in series eleven. That's all you can say really.

The subplot with the immortal police officer Brendan in Ireland is mildly intriguing because we obviously have to speculate on how this ties into the plot in a broader sense but these scenes are ones we ultimately could have lived without. You actually get the impression though that Chris Chibnall the writer is more at home in sedate rural period Ireland than he is trying to write escapist science fiction! Ascension of the Cybermen is never anywhere near as good or exciting as you want it to be but it's by no means bad. In comparison to the Chibnall era as a whole, this is a fairly solid episode in that stuff is happening and we, as an audience, are modestly engaged. We can nitpick Ascension of the Cybermen into oblivion if we wanted to because there are some glaring flaws but we are never bored watching this and that surely is the most important thing.

We probably expect more of Ascension of the Cybermen than we get in the end because Chris Chibnall, the Doctor Who team, and the BBC really talked this two-part finale up. Maybe they just got our expectations too high and made us expect too much. Ascension of the Cybermen is consequently not something that knocks our socks off but it is a modestly promising way to go into the real finale. Ascension of the Cybermen is no great shakes compared to the best Doctor Who episodes produced since 2005 but compared to the episodes produced since Chris Chibnall took over it's probably in the top ten. Ultimately though, we probably hoped that Ascension of the Cybermen would be more memorable and thrilling than it ever quite manages to become. Ascension of the Cybermen is no classic but it's watchable enough.

THE TIMELESS CHILDREN (Director - Jamie Magnus Stone, Writer - Chris Chibnall)

The Master teleports the Doctor to Gallifrey and imprisons her in a Matrix. The Master intends to show the Doctor that she is not who she thinks she is. We've reached the end of series twelve. It's (ahem) time for The Timeless Children. Let's hear what Chris Chibnall had to say as The Timeless Children was close to transmission - "I can't tell you anything about this episode. The Timeless Child is mentioned as far back as The Ghost Monument [2018], and the final episode of this series is where some of those questions get answered. It's a huge, emotional finale with lots of Cybermen. And it runs for 65 minutes. It's both epic, and personal. This is what you're always looking for in a series finale – the way the big, universe-threatening story impacts on the personal lives of your characters. And categorically that's what's happening in this episode. Watch this episode live. Or as soon as you can."

Chibnall also promised a "blistering" performance from Jodie Whittaker and an ending that would leave Doctor Who fans reeling in shock and in need of a very strong cup of tea. I made up the bit about the cup of tea but Chibnall did say we would be left reeling in shock. It might be more accurate to say that Chibnall's finale didn't so much have the fanbase reeling in shock but instead needlessly divided them.

The Timeless Children is an absolute mess of a finale. You desperately want to enjoy this finale but there are so many problems it's hard to know where to start. Problem number one is that Sacha Dhawan as the Master is stretched far too thin in this finale. He's in it more than the Doctor and begins to become annoying in the end. Sacha Dhawan cranks it up to eleven as the Master here and plays him like an especially deranged version of the Joker. It's as if the director, writer, and editor deduced that Sacha Dhawan is the only charismatic member of this cast and so put him in practically every scene. There's a desperation to Dhawan's performance in The Timeless Children. It's as if he knows he is the only person who can keep this fiasco afloat.

The second problem is that the Doctor plays a very secondary role. Chibnall had promised us a "blistering" performance from Jodie but we see no evidence of this fabled "blistering" performance. The Doctor spends most of the episode tied up and patiently listening to the Master prattle on about the secret of the Timeless Child. That is not a blistering performance. That is simply a bored looking actor standing in an uncomfortable position listening to Sacha Dhawan endlessly waffle his way through expositional dialogue. You can almost picture Jodie asking how long until lunch as she stands there tied up in the matrix. It's the big season finale and she spends most of the time standing silently as someone else delivers half the dialogue in the script. If there is a word that means the exact opposite of blistering then that is how you would describe Jodie's performance. It is as far away from blistering as you can get.

There's a hilariously preposterous scene in this finale where Graham talks to Yaz and tells her what a remarkable person she is. This is Chris Chibnall desperately trying to convince himself and the audience that Yaz has been a remarkable character. It rings completely hollow. Half the time we completely forgot that Yaz was even in the show. The companions get pretty short shrift in the finale. They are thrown a few silly action scenes and the notion that they disguised themselves as Cybermen to escape (this is conveniently done offscreen) requires a suspension of disbelief that we don't manage to attain.

Let's now move onto the secret of the Timeless Child. The Timeless Child is revealed to be the Doctor. That is the big secret the Master has been hinting at since Spyfall. The Doctor began life as small girl from another realm. Then had endless regenerations before the Doctor we know ourselves appeared. William Hartnell has always been the first Doctor. Chris Chibnall has now retconned the origin of the Doctor so that Hartnell could be the six billionth Doctor now for all we know. And what exactly are the implications of this? What changes? Well, nothing really. The Doctor bounces back to her old self again remarkably quickly. There are no consequences whatsoever.

The showrunner can of course tinker with the lore of Doctor Who. You can unpick what has gone before. RTD destroyed Gallifrey, Moffat brought it back, Chibnall destroyed it again. The odd thing about Chibnall's Timeless Child arc is that it changes nothing. It all feels pointless and needlessly divisive. And if the Doctor is now some super powerful indestructible Golden Child from another realm doesn't that sort of ruin the character of the Doctor? The Doctor is supposed to be an eccentric Time Lord from Gallifrey not the Silver Surfer.

It also begs a number of pedantic questions. How come Clara didn't see any of these other gazillions of Doctors when she entered Matt Smith's timestream? Why has Ruth got a police box TARDIS? And so on. The Timeless Children reveal reminds you of that Bond film where someone thought it would be a great idea for Blofeld to be James Bond's brother. There are just times when you are simply amazed that a stupid idea actually makes it onto the screen. Well, Chris Chibnall is the man we can thank for the stupid idea here. I suppose as showrunner he had no one to tell him it was a stupid idea that would (pointlessly) irritate a good portion of the fanbase.

What of the rest of The Timeless Children? Ashad is shrunk by the Master - rendering him a useless villain with an unsatisfying end. The Cyber-Time Lords created by the Master are arguably the single silliest thing we've seen in Doctor Who (I know, there's probably a lot of competition for this but they are stupid all the same). The Doctor is also made to look like a coward by devolving her responsibility when it comes to detonating the death particle at the end. The Brendan suplot in Ireland is preposterously explained as a vague memory of the Doctor to explain her past. And finally, the Doctor returns to her TARDIS and is promptly arrested by the Judoon. Can anyone just enter the TARDIS willy nilly now? I thought it was supposed to be unbreachable.

The Timeless Children is a dreadfully underwhelming finale. There is so much effort here that leads to nothing. There's too much exposition and not enough consequences. The companions have nothing to do, the Doctor spends too much time reacting to a speech rather than doing anything, Sacha Dhawan's Master is made to outstay his welcome, and the Timeless Child reveal is an eye-roll of the highest order. This is a complete mess. It makes even the maddest RTD finales look like masterclasses in how to be concise.

The Timeless Children is a really strange episode. It feels at times like it hasn't been edited and is a collection of random scenes. The Timeless Child arc feels like a waste of our time in the end and even if you liked the revison of the Doctor's past this episode hardly feels like justification for having been teased for two whole seasons about the Timeless Child. You patiently wait for The Timeless Children to get really good but it never really does in the end. The main emotion you come away with is frustration.

If these last two episodes had been really good then series twelve could have been a fairly resounding success in artistic terms. However, the patchy nature of the second half of the season did dent some of the early optimism generated by Spyfall. That said though, series twelve is superior to series eleven. Series twelve, despite its missteps, is really what series eleven should have been more like.

I did not much care for the twist in The Timeless Children and many fans didn't like the twist either. However, I concede that many fans were also fine with the twist and it is, as we have noted, entirely up to the showrunner what he does with Doctor Who during his tenure. Doctor Who is a show that has an incredible universe and a fantastical concept. There is, you might argue, nothing there that is completely set in stone. Chris Chibnall clearly felt that he was making the Doctor more interesting by tinkering with the history of Gallifrey. Who knows, perhaps the subtext is supposed to be about adopted children or people who feel rootless and displaced.

The message of The Timeless Children, we might speculate, is that learning something unexpected about your past doesn't change who you are in the present and that this history only makes you stronger and richer in spirit. I think I could probably have lived with the Timeless Child twist if this finale had been a lot better as a viewing experience and cohesive story. As it stands though, it just feels like a tremendous anti-climax to have this story teased for so long and then for it to ultimately play out in such an underwhelming fashion.

REVOLUTION OF THE DALEKS (Director - Lee Haven Jones, Writer - Chris Chibnall)

Revolution of the Daleks was a New Year's Day special (I really disliked the Sunday/New Year's Day combo for Chibnall's Who - I'm glad that Russell T Davies went back to Saturday/Christmas Day) and picks up after the events of the twelfth series finale, where the Doctor was incarcerated by the Judoon. Meanwhile, on Earth, her friends Yaz, Ryan, and Graham find themselves dealing with the aftermath of the Doctor's disappearance. As they are struggling to move on, they uncover a plot involving Daleks disguised as security drones.

Revolution of the Daleks is a middling sort of episode which is neither gratingly bad nor especially good. It just sits there in a fairly forgettable middle ground and is the sort of episode you completely forget about almost as soon as you've watched it. This is strange really because not only is it a New Year's special it is also notable for the return of Captain Jack (who this time is a full part of the episode - as opposed to his glorified cameo in Fugitive of the Judoon) and the departure of Graham and Ryan. You can't help feeling that Revolution of the Daleks should have been a bit more memorable than it actually turns out to be in the end. There are plenty of ingredients in place here for a better episode than the one we actually get.

The plot seems to be a commentary on military style police forces - which seems a rather misplaced plot for a British show. The subtext about surveillance is certainly relevant though. There's certainly no lack of effort in Revolution of the Daleks with the Doctor in prison at the start and the redesigned Dalek shenanigans at the end. Chibnall's script clearly wants this episode to be big and fun but the execution leaves it as something that never quite hits the bullseye. The return of Chris Noth's Jack Robertson character will elicit not much more than a shrug from anyone still trying to forget Arachnids in the UK and Harriet Walter's PM and Nathan Stewart-Jarrett's scientist both feel a trifle underfleshed. You always feel like Chibnall was trying to build up Jack Robertson into some big supervillain who was going to take over the world or something. This actually turned out to be his last appearance in the show though.

Revolution of the Daleks does at least have John Barrowman to lend a bit of spark as Captain Jack. To the credit of Jodie Whittaker, she works well with Barrowman and isn't overshadowed by his cheeky brand of charisma (which is shrewdly toned down by Barrowman in light of his age and being in a more staid and less campy era of Who this time around). Jack spends a lot of time with Yaz and gets some nice moments of reflection and a few action set-pieces. The special effects in the jail escape are a bit dodgy but it is nice anyway to see that Jack came up with an elaborate plan to get the Doctor out of space jail.

The only quibble you might have about Jack here is that his departure at the end feels oddly low-key. He just sort of disappears (he is apparently off to catch up with Gwen from Torchwood - just in case you think I might have fallen asleep and missed that bit). One problem this special is always battling is the unavoidable fact that the Daleks probably need a bit of a rest and are becoming too over familiar. It simply isn't a big deal anymore in the show to wheel them out as the villains anymore. The same thing happened in Star Trek when they kept bringing the Borg back. In the end even the greatest monsters lose some mystique if we become too familiar with them or see them too often.

You really need to give the Daleks a break and then come up with a way to make them more interesting again. Revolution of the Daleks never really finds a way to make the Daleks exciting or scary. It is just, for better or worse, a fairly bog standard Dalek themed adventure. There's a lot of silly stuff at the end although some of the sets are quite nice. At the very least though, Revolution of the Daleks is not boring in the way that series eleven was. It ambles along in brisk fashion and passes the time.

As is often the case though, Chris Chibnall's plot does not stand up to close inspection. By this stage of his run on Doctor Who, Chibnall is just throwing in as much crazy stuff as he can and then coming up with sci-fi gobbleygook to explain everything at the end. A problem with the globetrotting crazy Doctor Who scripts Chibnall was turning in at this time is the direction, budgets, and production was seldom up to making them.

This episode bids farewell to Graham and Ryan. While it might be stretching things to say this an emotional rollercoaster (we still feel like we hardly know these characters despite spending two seasons with them!), Tosin Cole does get a few nice moments near the end. Poor old Bradley Walsh is rather ill served by this episode as he barely features in it. Maybe he was shooting something else at the time? It seems a shame as Walsh was actually the best thing about the Jodie era. By the end of series twelve we don't really know Graham or Ryan or Yaz much more than we did at the start.

And the Doctor's interactions with these companions still feel oddly sterile and removed. There is no convincing bonding in Chibnall's era between the Doctor and the people who share the TARDIS. By the end of The Church on Ruby Road, Ncuti Gatwa's Doctor was hugging Millie Gibson's Ruby. David Tennant's Doctor kisses (in a platonic way) and hugs Donna Noble in the 60th anniversary specials. In the Chris Chibnall era of Who the interaction between Jodie's Doctor and the companions feels weird in comparison. There is never any physical contact or believable easygoing banter between the Doctor and the companions.

Revolution of the Daleks suffers somewhat from being a sequel to Resolution (an episode that most people can barely remember) and also by being a tad predictable. Nothing that happens here comes as a great surprise and as usual everything is wrapped up a bit too easily in the end. Revolution of the Daleks is nowhere near as bad as the worst episodes of the Chibnall era but still manages to be fairly average when compared to the best NuWho episodes. Still, at the very least it is watchable and John Barrowman's mere presence does lift it up a few notches and remind us of how past companions were frequently a lot more charismatic and interesting than the companions in the Chibnall era. The main problem with Revolution of the Daleks is that it lacks emotional weight and any sort of gravitas. It's all just a trifle too middle of the road and breezy for its own good.

SERIES 13 - FLUX

THE HALLOWEEN APOCALYPSE (Director - Jamie Magnus Stone, Writer - Chris Chibnall)

The Halloween Apocalypse is the first part of Jodie's third series - which was designated Doctor Who: Flux. "Der Flux," as the Toymaker might say. There were six episodes in the Flux arc - which told one long story and then after that we got three specials to end this era of Doctor Who. Doctor Who was in serious trouble around this time due to the pandemic and budget cuts. Chris Chibnall said the show was actually axed at one point and he and Jodie were offered other work. They decided though to stick with Doctor Who and managed to get the go ahead for Flux. To the credit of Chibnall, despite all the problems, he reacted by trying to do something ambitious in telling one big story. And this was surely playing to his strengths too because Chibnall's long form story work on Broadchurch was a lot better than his episodic work on Doctor Who.

The Halloween Apocalypse is a fairly decent start for the Flux arc. It isn't perfect and it has that wonkiness which pervades the Chibnall era (by 'wonkiness' I mean that nagging sense you often have during the Chibnall era that the acting, special effects, pacing, editing, and scripts could and probably should be better) but it has a bit of energy and zip to it (always welcome after the snoozefest of series eleven). Some people seemed to really dislike the Flux episodes but I'm happy to defend them - or most of them anyway. You have to give Chibnall credit for changing gears and trying something slightly different - even in the midst of the difficult circumstances he found himself in.

Anyway, what is the plot of this episode you ask? The Doctor and Yaz are after Karvanista (Craige Els) - who is part of an alien race called the Lupari. Karvanista looks like that piano playing dog from the Muppet Show and talks like Les Dawson. Chibnall has gone bonkers and embraced some craziness. And you know what? I don't mind at all. If this crazy version of Chris Chibnall had come out of the starting blocks in series eleven then at least we wouldn't have been so bored.

There is a lot happening in this episode, maybe too much, but it does at least keep things moving. It turns out that the Lupari are actually trying to rescue humans from Earth before a mysterious planet destroying entity called the Flux rolls in. The Flux is a very Star Trek type plot device. It's a lazy plot device if truth be told but it can be an effective plot device. You get the impression that Chris Chibnall came up with the Flux as this big broad vague MacGuffin for the story but then never actually got around to the fine details and just sort of made it up as he went along.

We meet a mysterious woman in this episode named Claire (Annabel Scholey) who seems to know the Doctor. The Doctor though doesn't know Claire. Meanwhile, a powerful entity named Swarm (Sam Spruell) escapes from imprisonment by the Divison. Sontarans and a Weeping Angel feature too. Oh, and I almost forgot that we get introduced to Dan Lewis (John Bishop). Dan is an unpaid Liverpudlian museum guide who doesn't like soup and often forgets to get himself anything for dinner so is at constant risk of starving to death. Dan is also being pursued by Karvanista and ends up being rescued by the Doctor. John Bishop as Dan is basically the replacement for Bradley Walsh in the show. John Bishop is not Sir Laurence Olivier in the old thesping department but he is likeable and makes a decent enough companion. I did enjoy the banter between Dan and Karvanista.

The Halloween Apocalypse and the Flux arc is probably the sort of thing that Chris Chibnall should have done right at the start of his tenure on Doctor Who. It isn't perfect and probably won't be for all tastes but this is a lot more entertaining than insomnia cures like The Tsuranga Conundrum and Demons of the Punjab. There is an unavoidable sense here that Chibnall is flinging as much stuff at the wall as possible in the hope that some of it will stick but even if you see this as a sign of desperation this approach is perfectly fine by me because the worst sin of series eleven is that it was boring. It was a dull watch where nothing much seemed to happen. Chibnall has finally seemed to realise that the version of Doctor Who he gave us in series eleven was neither exciting nor memorable at all.

The Halloween Apocalypse has its problems but at least you won't be bored watching it. Doctor Who is not a show where you should be bland and middle of the road. It is a show where you have licence to be as crazy as you want. Now, you might argue that Davies and Moffat sometimes fumbled the landings of their respective craziness and didn't always hit the target. But they also made some great entertaining television too. They did this because they were trying. They were ambitious. They were doing everything they could to give you entertaining stories and big finales. Chris Chibnall is finally swinging for the fences by this stage of his time on Doctor Who. He's trying to hit sixes. Chibnall doesn't always connect and he's being stumped from time to time but at least he's trying. He's finally on the front foot.

One other thing about the Flux arc that is refreshing is that the 'messaging' (for want of a better phrase) has been toned down. None of these episodes are preachy or have some clunky attempt to shoehorn in an obvious social message. Science fiction is a perfect vehicle to lace in a message or subtext. The trick is to lace this message naturally into an entertaining story. You don't, as Chibnall did too often on Who, present a boring story and then suddenly stop so that a character can tell the audience what the message is. Robocop is about corporate greed and uncaring out of control capitalism. The Day the Earth Stood Still is about pacifism. Starship Troopers is about fascism, brainwashing, propaganda, and the madness of war. These are all very entertaining films where we understand the message without feeling as if we are being patronised.

There is a good supporting cast in The Halloween Apocalypse with Jacob Anderson, Steve Oram, Rochenda Sandall, Annabel Scholey, and others. The main weakness with this episode is that there is a lot of info dumping and quite often you don't have the faintest idea what is going on on. It isn't the most coherent of stories. This is mostly explained though by the fact that this is merely the first part of one long story. The episode looks pretty good too - though it could probably have done without a ludicrous CGI comedy sequence at the start where the Doctor and Yaz escape from Karvanista. The Halloween Apocalypse is no NuWho classic but by the standards of the Chris Chibnall era is at least diverting and watchable.

WAR OF THE SONTARANS (Director - Jamie Magnus Stone, Writer - Chris Chibnall)

War of the Sontarans is the second part of the six episode Flux arc and it isn't too bad at all. I would have this sneaking into my top ten Chibnall/Jodie era episodes. Most of the episode takes place during the Crimean War but time has been altered and the British are fighting the Sontarans. Yaz encounters Yinder in the Temple of Atropos on the planet Time and ends up as the mercy of the villain Swarm. Meanwhile, Dan ends up back in present day Liverpool and finds that the timeline has been altered and the Sontarans now rule the planet. Suffice to say, an awful lot happens in this episode. Not a lot of it makes sense but things are happening and Chibnall's version of Doctor Who is finally propulsive and moving forward. You could say that Chris Chibnall finally seems to be getting the hang of this Doctor Who lark.

As with the other early parts of Flux, War of the Sontarans is confusing at times and does betray a palpable sense of desperation on the part of Chibnall in that he knows the clock is ticking down on his tenure and he needs a strong finish to make up for the early stumbles. The episode works quite well though and is really the sort of thing Chibnall should have done right from the start of his run on the show. This episode has quite a nice dual quality in that it is a historical but a historical with a crazy sci-fi twist. So we get to meet real people like Mary Seacole and Joseph Williamson - only in unusual circumstances.

War of the Sontarans reminds me of the type of episode that Mark Gatiss would write during his time on the show. Gatiss wasn't my favourite Doctor Who writer by any stretch of the imagination and a lot of his episodes were a bit dull. However, he would often have an interesting idea where he'd infuse science fiction into some specific historical period or event. Chibnall does the same sort of thing here. War of the Sontarans has a good atmosphere although budgetary constraints mean that a lot of the battle going on happens offscreen. There are still some decent setpieces though and Chibnall is getting a bit better by now at incorporating all his characters into a story and giving them something to do. Yaz has more scenes now that Graham and Ryan are no longer around but still isn't registering much as a character.

You'd have to say that Yaz was one of the biggest failures of the Chibnall era in that she was there from start to finish but just ended up as this weird blank of a character who we completely forgot about the moment the Chibnall era ended. Maybe it might be nice if one day Yaz made another appearance in the show with a different writer and Doctor. It would certainly be interesting to see Mandip Gill have another crack at the part in different circumstances and with better scripts.

One thing that is quite nice about the Flux arc is that it often separates the Doctor from the companions and so this allows Jodie have to have more of a solo spotlight - which is long overdue in the Chibnall era (festooned with a TARDIS full of companions as it was most of the time). Jodie does some decent work in the Flux episodes and her performance overall is better than the acting she did in series eleven. Series eleven was so lackadaisical it beggared belief and Chibnall seems to have learned from that and made his version of Who more energetic with lots of things happening and crazy twists.

It doesn't always land (and we already fear that Chibnall is probably not going to land the ending of Flux down the road) in War of the Sontarans but, generally, this is a hell of a lot more entertaining than glacial tap water like Demons of the Punjab and Rosa. War of the Sontarans is not Heaven Sent but it is an episode that is well up to par. It is passable, very watchable, and not a chore to sit through. The audience is having a decent time and the story is interesting. That's all we wanted going into series eleven but didn't get. It might be a bit late in the day but Chris Chibnall is clearly getting better at doing Doctor Who.

There are though things to nitpick in this episode - like the fact the Sontarans are still a bit cartoonish rather than scary. Vinder is also a rather dull and forgettable character. There was speculation that this role was supposed to be Captain Jack but then got changed to a completely new character named Vinder when John Barrowman's past conduct on the show came under scrutiny (you know what I'm talking about here, you probably don't need me to dredge this up). Anyway, Flux definitely would have been better and more fun if it had Captain Jack in it instead of Vinder. There's probably no doubt about that - unless of course you are a Doctor Who fan who got a bit tired of Captain Jack back when he was a regular.

War of the Sontarans is a trifle scattershot but it has some energy to it and Jodie is much better in episodes like this where the Doctor is essentially having to figure things out on her own. Jodie's Doctor was a bit annoying at the best of times running around with the TARDIS team like a supply teacher on a field trip. When you isolate her Doctor though and put her in a tricky situation you get a glimpse of the more interesting Doctor that Jodie could have been if the writing and structure of the show had been better. Jodie has been really good in other things both before and after Doctor Who so you would definitely say she was capable of more than the Chibnall era of Doctor Who allowed.

One other good thing about having one long arc like Flux is

that we get cliffhangers too - something which was sorely missed in series eleven. War of the Sontarans is, for want of a better phrase, a 'solid' episode of Doctor Who. It isn't amazing but it is perfectly decent for what it is and a lot better than some of the dreck served up in series eleven and even series twelve. I enjoy War of the Sontarans and think it is a pretty good episode.

ONCE, UPON TIME (Director - Azhur Saleem, Writer - Chris Chibnall)

Once, Upon Time is the third episode in the Flux arc. What is the plot of this episode you ask? Well, that's a good question and I wish I had an answer. After a very decent start, the Flux story basically goes nowhere in this slightly confusing all over the place wheel-spinning third episode. It's a shame really because you suspect a few people probably bailed out in frustration after this one and missed the better stuff to come. If that is the case I think that's somewhat unfair because while there are some weaker episodes in Flux there is nothing that is outrageously bad relative to others episode (in the fashion that Orphan 55 was shockingly and inexplicably dreadful relative to the strong Spyfall opening of series twelve).

The Flux arc is just about as consistent as Chris Chibnall ever got on Doctor Who. It isn't perfect but at least you don't get whiplash from the jarring inconsistency - as in other parts of his stewardship. As we noted in the preface, a classic example of this was when Chibnall produced two interesting and well made 2022 specials but somehow contrived to turn out the abysmal Legend of the Sea Devils in the middle of them. Anyway, in Once, Upon Time the Daleks, Cybermen, and Sontarans have taken over most of the universe and the Doctor hides Dan, Yaz, and Vinder in the past.

Chris Chibnall's endless deployment of the Daleks and Cybermen is unavoidably a little tiresome by now. I think the Cybermen could really do with a very long rest from Doctor

Who after Chibnall literally ran them into the ground. Too much of this episode deals with Vinder's backstory and this is a bit of a slog in the end because we don't really care that much about Vinder at all as a character. I could happily have lived without any backstory for Vinder.

Vinder's lover Bel (Thaddea Graham - giving an atrocious performance) is also introduced in this episode. She's searching for Vinder among the stars. Personally speaking I didn't care about Bel either and would have been perfectly fine with Bel and Vinder being written out of these episodes altogether. The wooden acting by some of the supporting players in this episode gives us some unwelcome season eleven flashbacks. That's just me though. Maybe the majority of people liked Vinder and Bel. I just found their romance subplot a trifle corny and inwardly groaned whenever they threatened to get too much screen time. .

Once, Upon Time does sort of make sense if you think about it but the concepts here are rather vague (space v time) and Chibnall's kitchen sink approach seems designed to mask the fact that his plot is basically a load of old nonsense thrown together in the hope that no one will notice the joins. The special effects in this episode are often on the dodgy side but occasionally in a charming sort of way. Jo Martin's Fugitive Doctor makes a brief appearance and there are all manner of monsters and creatures from the show's history. It is somewhat ironic that series eleven was a clean slate where Chibnall tried to eschew the show's iconic villains in order to do his own thing. By this stage in the Chibnall era though he's desperately throwing in every single old villain he can think of in an attempt to make this show interesting again.

This is a wise tactic really because Chibnall's own villains just don't cut the mustard. They are terrible. If you were the showrunner of Doctor Who and got a script from Chris Chibnall the first thing you would do is take out his villain and replace it with something else. Flying tea towels, the time travelling racist who looks like a reject from Grease, the CGI

Gremlin who eats metal, Tim Shaw. These are, by any standards, a rather forgettable and uninspired collection of baddies. Chibnall had no choice but to dip into the Doctor Who back catalogue because he clearly can't come up with classic monsters of his own.

Despite the Flux arc only being six episodes long, Once, Upon Time does actually feel a bit like a filler episode. It feels weaker and less propulsive than the first two episodes - despite all the huffing and puffing. Still, at least in the Flux episodes the companions are put in a bit of peril. We never really got much of a sense they were ever under threat in series eleven because the season was so flat and unengaging. Even when they were being chased by giant spiders or about to be killed by the rotation of a sun we never really cared or felt the sense of danger the story was trying to project.

In the Moffat era of Doctor Who we felt a sense of danger for the companions. We knew that travelling with the Doctor was a risky line of work. We always feared that something horrible could happen to these companions - and it often did. They were nabbed by Sleeping Angels, turned into Cybermen, left behind by the Doctor to grow old alone, had their memories wiped, and more besides. Chibnall, to his credit, does inject more danger into Flux for the characters than previously on the show.

Once, Upon Time is a bit too manic and confusing for its own good and never really finds any firm footing. It is the weakest part of Flux at this stage - though the following episode would thankfully be much better. One of the disappointing things about Chibnall is that he has experience with cliffhangers and long form television plotting but he eschewed these elements when he took control of Doctor Who. It was but one of many baffling decisions in series eleven. The best thing about Flux though is cliffhangers are back. In a sense then you can be more forgiving of Once, Upon Time because it is essentially a cog in a bigger unfolding story.

VILLAGE OF THE ANGELS (Director - Jamie Magnus Stone, Writer - Chris Chibnall, Maxine Alderton)

Village of the Angels is the fourth part of the Flux arc and one of the best episodes of the Chibnall era. I would have this in my top 5 Chibnall/Jodie era episodes. Like the season twelve episode The Haunting of Villa Diodati, it was co-written by Chibnall and Maxine Alderton. It's a shame really that Maxine Alderton didn't do a lot more writing on Doctor Who during the Chibnall era because the quality of the show seems to suddenly improve whenever her name is on a script. Alderton has written many of the episodes of the soap opera Emmerdale (and was the script editor on that show) but she clearly has an aptitude for science fiction too.

In this episode, the Doctor, Yaz, and Dan find themselves trapped in the spooky mist hazed village of Medderton in 1967. Yaz and Dan join the search for a missing girl named Peggy while the Doctor chances upon a Professor Jericho (Kevin McNally) - who is conducting psychic research on Claire. Claire is the women who recognised the Doctor in the first part of Flux. This mystery all revolves around a rogue Weeping Angel - which will spell big trouble and peril for the Doctor, Claire, and Jericho.

Village of the Angels has a terrific sense of atmosphere and essentially becomes a siege episode in the end when the Angels seek to get into Professor Jericho's lab. There is a real sense of danger for the Doctor, Claire, and Jericho in this episode and we feel that danger too because the characters are well developed. It helps a lot that you have an old pro like Kevin McNally (no stranger to Doctor Who - he was in The Twin Dilemma many years ago) as Jericho and by the end of the episode McNally has made us care enough about Professor Jericho to want him to survive.

The Weeping Angels trying to infiltrate the house (and Claire!) make for a creepy and effective premise. What this episode shows is that you don't need numerous locations and daft CGI action setpieces to make a good episode of Doctor Who. As long as the concept, characters, and script is solid, a constrictive story like this can make its simplicity an advantage. The 1960s psychic research trappings are fun and there is a hook to keep us interested with the drip feed of information concerning the Doctor and Division. Village of the Angels also has a fantastic and memorable cliffhanger. If this was the type of episode that Chibnall that served up right from the start in series eleven then he wouldn't have got so much criticism and would be compared much more favourably with his predecessors.

It was the inconsistency more than anything which drove a lot of fans crackers with Chibnall's version of Doctor Who. The inability to put together a competent run of episodes without any clunkers. Flux isn't perfect and has some problems but it is much more engaging than series eleven and doesn't have awful clunkers like Orphan 55 and Praxeus weighing it down in the same fashion that series twelve did. Village of the Angels is laced with references to Who past and other sci-fi but it earns these references because it is a strong piece in its own right. These cosmic nightmarish events revolving around a mundane village evoke the work of John Wyndham and the concept of a place out of time that you can't escape from is rather Lovecraftian.

This is a very ghostly episode of Doctor Who and works very well as a behind the sofa chiller. The story has fun with the lore and abilities of the Weeping Angels and Jodie Whittaker comes into her own a bit more in episodes like this where the Doctor is separated. In the previous two series you would often come to dread the moment when Jodie and the 'fam' suddenly blustered into the narrative at the start but Jodie's Doctor, for my money at least, seems to work better when she's having to solve problems on her own and meeting new characters alone. Village of the Angels reminds one somewhat of the (decent enough) Moffat era story Hide but is more memorable than that episode.

The mystery of Peggy is not exactly difficult to predict in this episode but it is well done all the same and the concept of a village taken out of time and space is not only very errie but also very Doctor Who. By the way, Blaké Harrison has a guest spot in this episode and has a lot more luck than his old Inbetweeners co-star James Buckley. Harrison got Village of the Angels while poor old James Buckley was in Orphan 55.

The overall Flux story doesn't really stand up to close inspection if you think about it too much but then the same can be said of most Doctor Who stories and it doesn't really matter in this case. The important thing is that, by the standards of the Chibnall era, Village of the Angels is great stuff. It is well directed, the FX are good, the guest actors are good, the atmosphere is great, and - best of all - the Weeping Angels are scary. This episode is about as good as the Chibnall era ever got. It's just a shame that he couldn't maintain this standard on a more consistent basis.

SURVIVORS OF THE FLUX (Director - Azhur Saleem, Writer - Chris Chibnall)

Survivors of the Flux is the fifth part of the Doctor Who: Flux arc and suffers quite a bit from having to follow Village of the Angels - which was one of the best episodes in the whole of the Chris Chibnall era. Survivors of the Flux has a lot happening but it still comes across as a bit dull at times and worst of all is the fact that the Doctor spends most of this episode confused and asking questions. It's never a great idea to depict the Doctor as clueless because the Doctor's superpower is intelligence. However, that is exactly what Chris Chibnall does here. It is similar to how Chibnall had the Doctor constantly tied up and confused in The Timeless Children.

One thing that the Chibnall era probably could have done with is a Heaven Sent style episode where Jodie was the only actor onscreen. That would have been very interesting and might have help cement Jodie much more in the role. There were so many companions in the first two series of Jodie's tenure that the Doctor sometimes felt like a supporting character rather than the undisputed lead.

In this episode, the Doctor is transported to meet the head of Division. Awsok (Barbara Flynn) reveals herself to be Tecteun - the Doctor's adoptive mother in Chibnall's new version of the Doctor's origins. Chibnall is doubling down on his Timeless Child concept. I'm not the biggest fan of this concept but we are just going to have to get used to it now because Russell T Davies has already made reference to it since he took the reins of Doctor Who from Chibnall. Though some fans were hoping the Timeless Child story would be overturned or simply ignored by the next producer this was unrealistic because Davies is obviously a friend of Chibnall and he's not going to brush Chibnall's big concept under the carpet and pretend it never happened.

Barbara Flynn is very good as Tecteun but this story thread does get a bit boring and it doesn't help matters that Jodie is basically required to look gormless and ask questions rather too much in this episode. You would definitely say this episode marks a dip in quality compared to Village of the Angels and the first two episodes in the Flux arc. It is more or less on a par with the third episode in that it is quite competent (as far as the Chibnall era goes) but not something that really grabs you very much or lingers in the memory for long afterwards.

Despite the fact that episodes like this don't live up to expectations, I find it difficult to be too harsh on the Flux arc because it is the sort of thing that Chibnall should have done from the start. Sure, not everyone enjoyed Flux and some found it a bit messy and incoherent, but at least it is swinging for the fences. Series eleven was interesting only in the way that it was a reboot but one with no teeth. The show changed a lot. We had a new female Doctor, a bigger TARDIS team, an eschewing of the history of Doctor Who and the angry lonely God angst of the character. Chibnall avoided classic villains and made the Doctor feel much more, well, human.

Chibnall seemed to want to make the show more simplistic in series eleven. The Doctor was more friendly and not weighed down by emotional baggage and the stories had a more educational feel. The pacing was more sedate and the new music felt more in the background than the (occasionally bombastic) scores by Murray Gold. None of these things were bad in theory. You might even say that some of them were interesting and understandable decisions. The problem is though that none of these decisions payed off in the end. Jodie's less complex nice new Doctor was bland and boring. The 'educational' stories were shallow and patronising. The TARDIS was too crowded. The new villains were pathetic. The new music was pleasant but forgettable.

It was a tame and strangely half-hearted reboot. There were no stakes to anything. Nothing happened. It was all too slow, too talky, and too safe. And worst of all, it was smug. It was very pleased with itself. One thing you can't accuse Flux of being is tame. Flux is bold. Chris Chibnall is not tiptoeing around the Doctor Who sandbox anymore. He's right there in the sandbox covered in sand and smashing all the toys up. The end result is a season (if we can call Flux a season) of Doctor Who that is much more watchable than series eleven. It's not perfect and we get some unwelcome series eleven flashbacks in its worst moments but Flux is often entertaining in a way that series eleven never was.

Dan, Yaz, and Jericho go on a world tour in this episode - which is sort of fun despite the trademark Chibnall era production wonkiness which plagues this show's attempts to be epic and far-flung. Chibnall's era of Doctor Who often looks a bit cheap and slapdash compared to the Moffatt era. The characters of Dan and Yaz actually work quite well together in Flux though despite the fact that Mandip Gill and John Bishop are not, with respect, what you would call master thespians. Professor Jericho remains a nice addition in Flux. I like a fair few of the supporting characters in Flux like Karvanista and Jericho.

This episode marks the return of Jemma Redgrave (who seems a bit bored here) as Kate Stewart. Craig Parkinson as the villain Prentis/Grand Serpent has embedded himself into UNIT so he can close it down and make the Earth more vulnerable. This plot thread is quite interesting but a bit drawn out. With all the characters coming and going and the universe ending (but not quite) shenanigans, Survivors of the Flux is a bit of a mess at the best of times but it is far from the worst of the Chibnall era. It is certainly one of the weakest links in the Flux arc and falls well short of the best series twelve episodes like Spyfall 1&2, Fugitive of the Judoon, and The Haunting of Villa Diodati, but it is still - The Woman Who Fell to Earth aside - more watchable than series eleven. Survivors of the Flux has some good stuff but it is terribly uneven too and somewhat dragged down by all the exposition and the depiction of the Doctor as a reactionary character who has no idea what is going on.

THE VANQUISHERS (Director - Azhur Saleem, Writer - Chris Chibnall)

The Vanquishers is the sixth and final part of the six episode Flux arc. It is probably the worst episode of the Flux arc and this is a shame really because parts of the Flux were very good and some of the best stuff that Chibnall has done on the show during his time running Doctor Who. The main problem with The Vanquishers is that it feels very underwhelming with no real consequences and everything wrapped up way too easily. It all feels very hollow and pointless.

Chibnall's kitchen sink approach to Flux, with all the characters and returning villains, has reaped a few dividends along the way but we always feared that Chibnall would stumble when it came to actually wrapping this thing up. That fear turns out to be more than justified here. To be fair to Chibnall it isn't as if he is alone in having this problem. Russell T Davies and Steven Moffat have both flubbed more than their fair share of endings too. Moffat even flubbed his endings to

Dracula and Sherlock.

The Vanquishers is just a bit of a mess really and nothing is wrapped up in a satisfactory fashion. A major problem in this last chapter of Flux is there is too much going on and too many characters. This means that some things are forgotten, not given sufficient time to be explained, or just wafted away with some gobbleygook technobabble dialogue.

By the end of this episode we have no idea what the exact consequences have actually been for the universe and we suspect that Chris Chibnall has no idea either. It's as if he hoped no one would think about it too much afterwards and we just forget all about by the time the next episode aired!

The Vanquishers moves at a hundred miles an hour but it still manages to be a bit dull because nothing seems to have any weight in the script. Nothing is given time to be absorbed. Even moments that should be affecting and moving like the death of Jericho and the Lupari's extinction are just rattled off with no reaction. Things that were teased earlier in Flux go nowhere, villains vanish, and the whole thing is preposterously convoluted to the point where none of it makes any sense and you just want it to end. You can give Chris Chibnall credit for being ambitious with Flux and you can give him credit for some of the decent episodes it spawned. You can't though give him much credit I'm afraid for The Vanquishers. In the end you wish this episode had been written by someone else.

The mechanics of the writing with Yaz and Dan in Flux is sometimes odd. We don't feel as if we know these characters much better at the end of Flux than we did at the start. They don't have much development. The relationship between the Doctor and the companions is also weird in the Chibnall era. We are constantly told that they are the 'fam' and yet we see little evidence of any bonding or personal chemistry between them. We saw that Ryan wanted to escape his boring job in a warehouse and Graham wanted something to distract him from the death of Grace but why is Yaz in the TARDIS? What is she running away from? I thought she had a career as a police officer? Is Yaz only in the TARDIS because she loves the Doctor? I have no idea because none of this is ever resolved. Yaz and Dan become increasingly marginal as Flux wears on - which feels like a shame.

I liked the Flux arc more than a lot people. It was patchy but there were a couple of really good episodes and most of it was a hell of a lot more entertaining than series eleven and series twelve rubbish like Orphan 55. I liked Karvanista, I liked Jericho, I like Swarm & Azure at first as the villains, and I liked Dan as the new companion too.

There was a lot to like but in the end it collapsed in on itself and seemed to be missing a coherent and satisfying ending. Maybe it might have been better if Flux had lost a few characters and plots and just been four episodes long or something. Maybe they could have got rid of Bel and Vinder and Tecteun.

The Vanquishers is a headache inducing finale to the Flux story and a bit of a damp squib. You can see that Chibnall was really trying with this episode. He is plainly trying to make it fast and fun and crazy. That effort though comes off as desperation at times in The Vanquishers as if it is all designed to distract us from the fact there ultimately wasn't an awful lot underpinning this story besides some broad generic concepts. The Vanquishers is nowhere near as bad as the worst episodes in Chibnall's Doctor Who but it isn't very good either.

It seems that Chris Chibnall overreached himself in the end with the Flux episodes and couldn't quite make a smooth landing after a very promising beginning. You have to give him a lot of credit for trying though. It is admirable that he put together this big bold crazy story arc and managed to get it produced at a time when things were exceptionally difficult for the television industry and the future of Doctor Who was by no means certain. Although the Chris Chibnall era of Doctor Who got a lot of criticism (much of it deserved in my opinion as my reviews of series eleven would indicate) I suspect that it may not be regarded as an outlier or black sheep of NuWho quite so much once the dust settles on it and it fades into the past.

All eras of Doctor Who had had some disappointing episodes and some very good episodes and some middling episodes. The main problem with the Chibnall era is that he gave us a few too many disappointing and middling episodes. He was capable of good episodes but we didn't quite get enough of them. When it comes to the six Flux episodes, I'd say that two of them are very good, a couple of them are passable, and then a couple of them are a bit middling and underwhelming. There are no out and out disasters though. There's no Orphan 55 or Arachnids in the UK here.

On the whole then you'd say that the Flux arc, a few quibbles aside, was a success as far as the Chibnall era goes and the most consistent season of the show he turned in during his tenure. Flux could have easily turned out to be a complete disaster but it was pretty decent in the end. It was fairly entertaining, introduced some good new characters, and in Village of the Angels had a memorable spooky episode which Moffat or Davies would have been proud of. All in all then, we can give Chris Chibnall plenty of credit for producing Flux in difficult and testing circumstances.

2022 SPECIALS

EVE OF THE DALEKS (Director - Annetta Laufer, Writer - Chris Chibnall)

Eve of the Daleks was the first of the three specials which marked the end of the Jodie/Chibnall era. It was broadcast on New Year's Day in 2022. After the events of the Flux, the Doctor, Yaz, and Dan find themselves in a storage warehouse in Manchester run by a woman named Sarah (Aisling Bea). Sarah is visted by a man named Nick (Adjani Salmon) who has a crush on her. A Dalek appears and wreaks havoc but the TARDIS resetting itself creates a repeating time loop. This creates a Groundhog Day situation where the Doctor and the other characters must find a way to defeat the Dalek. There is a twist though because with each loop the time shortens - leaving them less time to carry out a successful plan.

Eve of the Daleks is hardly original (we've seen a time loop plot like this in countless episodes of Star Trek let alone other science fiction and fantasy shows) and it feels a bit tiresome for Chibnall to (ahem) wheel the Daleks out YET again for a special but this is an episode that works reasonably well and holds up to a repeat viewing a lot better than most of the Chibnall era Who stuff. The first time you watch Eve of the Daleks you feel a bit disappointed initially at how cheap and unambitious it feels with the constrictive setting and drab location. It feels like a bottle episode designed to avoid spending any money.

However, this actually works to the strength of Eve of the Daleks because the focus is simply on the concept and atmosphere. All too frequently during his era on the show Chris Chibnall would write some overblown globetrotting story which fell flat on its face when it actually hit the screen but Eve of the Daleks is more digestible by dint of being a deliberately small scale story. It feels like Chibnall knew he wasn't going to have much time or money to make this episode so he came up with something that didn't require locations or too many special effects.

Eve of the Daleks is all the better for this simple approach and works a lot better than globetrotting nonsense like Praxeus or Legend of the Sea Devils. The Daleks in this special are Executioner Daleks and have extra (machine) guns. The Dalek shenanigans in this episode work quite well as this is a stripped down story that has a tight focus. All the same though, you definitely feel like the Daleks need a break from the show even while watching this. It should feel like a big deal when the Daleks show up in Doctor Who but it never does in the Chibnall era. To be fair to Chibnall the Daleks had stopped being a big deal long before he took over running the show.

As for problems with this episode, well, the main one is that some people are going to find this episode a bit dull. It works for what it is but all the same it isn't the most exciting piece of television. Aisling Bea and Pauline McLynn are quite good as the guest stars though their characters do come off as weird - which is a fault of Chibnall's writing rather than the actors. There is, as usual with Chibnall, too much exposition and his attempts at humour continue to fall flat. Another quibble one might have with Eve of the Daleks is that the Doctor seems remarkably chipper after the universe shattering events of Flux. In fact, she was planning to go to the beach. I'm imagine brooding in the TARDIS for a bit would be more in keeping with the character of the Doctor than sunbathing.

Jodie's version of the Doctor feels in manic mode in Eve of the Daleks, endlessly waving her Sonic around and explaining everything to the companions as if they are stupid. Chibnall's approach is baffling in the way that he stripped the Doctor of most of the traits that make the Doctor the Doctor. Jodie's Doctor has no sense of an inner life or past. No sense of anger or sorrow. No sense of intrigue or danger. No sense of being an ancient soul or an alien outsider. Chibnall has literally written his version of the Doctor as a daffy lass from Huddersfield.

The defence of Jodie Whittaker is that Chris Chibnall did her no favours with these scripts. Meryl Streep would probably have struggled to lend much depth to the dialogue Jodie had to grapple with.

John Bishop continues to be likeable as Dan and is proving to be a fairly clever choice of replacement for Bradley Walsh. Chibnall's habit of shoehorning some 'worthy' drama into his Who scripts arrives here when Dan tells Yaz that she should let the Doctor know about her feelings for her. The dialogue isn't terribly good in this scene and Chibnall is fooling us in a sense because he is hinting at a development that surely can't come to anything or be expanded and resolved because there are only two episodes left!

It is quite good fun to see the Doctor and the characters die but come back when the loop resets itself - though I can't be the only person who noticed that the Dalek seems to be a terrible shot even with the gatling gun. Eve of the Daleks is definitely a bit rough around the edges and lacks the polish that you came to expect in the Davies and Moffat eras but it is a fairly solid episode. It plays like a mid-season episode rather than a special but Eve of the Daleks is not bad at all and better than the vast majority of season eleven. The fan reception to Eve of the Daleks was quite interesting in that some thought it was one of the best Chibnall stories and others thought it was absolutely tedious. There didn't seem to be much middle ground - though overall the episode got pretty good critic reviews.

Eve of the Daleks works quite well coming straight after Flux because Flux was (deliberately) overstuffed and had lots of crazy stuff happening. It had dozens of characters and locations. Eve of the Daleks works as a nice change of pace after Flux thanks to its constrictive setting and minimal slate of characters. Eve of the Daleks also has minimal plot - just a basic concept. Usually with episodes of Doctor Who we grumble when there isn't much of a plot but in Eve of the Dalkeks that's the whole point and the key to enjoying the episode.

Eve of the Daleks can be nitpicked and it doesn't feel much like a special but, by the standards of the Chris Chibnall era, it isn't bad. It's a passable episode with an interesting concept and the fact that the constrictive story seems tailored to mitigate production issues is something that works to its advantage. I would have Eve of the Daleks just about sneaking into the back end of my top ten Chibnall/Jodie era episodes. It isn't Heaven Sent but it is a fairly solid Doctor Who story.

LEGEND OF THE SEA DEVILS (Directed by Haolu Wang, Written by Ella Road and Chris Chibnall)

Hurrah. The Sea Devils are finally back. Hold on, not so fast. Dampen those celebrations down. The Sea Devils might be back but sadly they've been lumbered with one of the worst Doctor Who episodes ever made. The plot has Madam Ching (Crystal Yu) raiding a village and releasing the Sea Devil Marsissus from a stone statue. The Doctor, Yaz, and Dan arrive to investigate. Madame Ching, in case you were wondering, was a prominent pirate during the early 19th century in the South China Sea.

Legend of the Sea Devils is strictly amateur hour. The story makes no sense and is filled with more holes than a garden invaded by a million moles. The special effects are atrocious (and often appear unfinished) and the acting is abysmal. This is an episode where you get the distinct impression the cast would rather be doing something else. Legend of the Sea Devils was a difficult production by all accounts due to the pandemic and it really shows. This 'special' is conspicuously on the short side at 47 minutes and the editing is bizarre to say the least. It feels like there are whole scenes missing and one suspects that insufficient coverage was produced. Legend of the Sea Devils makes your average CBBC show look like Game of Thrones. This is truly the scrapings from the bottom of the Chibnall barrel.

The story in Legend of the Sea Devils never makes any sense and the pirate antics of Dan are preposterous even for a science fiction fantasy show. When we first met Dan he was incapable of buying something for his dinner and didn't seem to realise that human beings have to eat food. Now he's suddenly an Olympic swimmer, expert swordsman, and knows how to steer a pirate ship. Whoever had the idea of making the new Sea Devils episode a panto pirate caper should probably be forced to walk the plank and have raw seaweed for their dinner. I think there should be a new clause in any contract for Doctor Who writers where it stipulates that on no account should they ever write a pirate themed story. The Curse of the Black Spot with Matt Smith was fairly forgettable and Legend of the Sea Devils is a hundred times worse.

Legend of the Sea Devils reminds one a lot of Orphan 55 in that it feels so slapdash and unfinished you can barely believe it was even deemed fit for transmission. The Sea Devils are completely neutralised by mere dint of being in this dreadful episode and as a consequence come off as bland generic monster villains. The look of the Sea Devils feels generic too. They lack the sinister unblinking unfathomable menace of their Classic Who incarnation. This episode looks awful too. It looks like a show made in the 1990s rather a show made in 2022. It is utterly baffling how a prestige show like Doctor Who can be this bad. It plays like they came up with this idea for a big swashbuckling adventure romp but then didn't have the money or the expertise to actually make the episode properly.

Ella Road, who co-wrote this episode, was once called Britain's most promising playwright. Heaven knows what Ella Road must have thought when she watched this episode. I'll wager the finished product on the screen was nothing like the one she imagined in her head when she was writing this. It's a shame really that this episode came so late in Jodie's run because much (if not all) of what came after series eleven was an improvement but Legend of the Sea Devils is an absolute disaster in the vein of clunkers like Orphan 55 and The

Tsuranga Conundrum.

By now the show has established that Yaz is attracted to the Doctor. We get the sense that the Doctor is attracted to Yaz too but is afraid to do anything about it. Therefore this little subplot is never resolved. That's fine by me because I prefer the Doctor to be an asexual character above and beyond all of this and a character who doesn't have crushes on companions. The problem with this thread though is that it involves a lot of us being told what an amazing and extraordinary person Yaz is and this rings hollow because Yaz, alas, is one of the most underwritten and least memorable characters in Doctor Who history. When the Chibnall era ended and Russell T Davies brought back Donna Noble for the anniversary specials did anyone honestly miss not having Yaz around anymore?

Legend of the Sea Devils mostly takes place on obvious soundstages and the dodgy CGI and lack of extras makes it all look and feel cheap. The action scenes are dreadful and embarrassing. I gather that this episode was supposed to be part of a series thirteen which events nixed. When it finally went into production it was hobbled by the pandemic and also a script that plainly needed more work. This episode wants to be a jaunty popcorn blockbuster style romp but it is executed in such incompetent fashion that it simply falls flat on its face. It has terrible dialogue, terrible direction, terrible acting performances, and despite all the huffing and puffing it is incredibly boring to sit through. We also get a by now familiar and lazy Chibnall trope where a character sacrifices themselves for the Doctor.

There isn't much to say about Legend of the Sea Devils except to say this is a complete fiasco of an episode. The costumes are nice I suppose - you can give them that. What this special illustrates more than anything is a salient weakness of the Chibnall era - the maddening inconsistency. Just when you think he's finally turned turned a corner and is starting to get the hang of Doctor Who he suddenly pulls out an episode so bad you can barely believe what you are watching. Legend of the Sea Devils is an unbelievably shoddy and inept piece of television and surely one of the worst episodes of NuWho since the show came back from its Michael Grade sanctioned limbo.

THE POWER OF THE DOCTOR (Director - Jamie Magnus Stone, Writer - Chris Chibnall)

The era of Jodie Whittaker and Chris Chibnall came to an end with The Power of the Doctor - the last of their 2022 specials. At the end of this episode, Jodie regenerates into David Tennant and the baton is handed once again to Russell T Davies (who was obviously returning for his second stint as showrunner). Going into this final episode there was a degree of fan scepticism due to the fact that this was not only Jodie's final episode but would also feature the return of the Master and the companions Tegan and Ace.

How could Chris Chibnall possibly wrap up the Jodie era in a satisfactory way and produce a coherent and decent episode in what sounded like an overstuffed final special? Given Chibnall's track record when it came to finales one can understand why some feared the worst. Expectations were also unavoidably lowered by the abysmal penultimate special Legend of the Sea Devils. Going into this final special you probably would have got long odds that Chris Chibnall could pull this off and go out on a high note.

Amazingly though, for once, Chris Chibnall proved the doubters wrong because The Power of the Doctor is actually a lot of fun and one of the very best episodes of his era. It is also a very moving episode at times with some poignant dialogue and plenty of big surprises. In truth, the plot of The Power of the Doctor doesn't really stand up to close scrutiny and yet AGAIN we get Cybermen wheeled out (or CyberMasters if you prefer) but there is so much that is enjoyable in this episode that it doesn't really matter. Sacha Dhawan seems to be having a whale of a time as the Master and Sophie Aldred slips back into the role of Ace as if she's never been away. Janet Fielding is also good as Tegan Jovanka. This is a nostalgia driven episode that you'd have to have a heart of stone not to enjoy. In fact, I would even argue that The Power of the Doctor is better than the last episode that both Matt Smith and Peter Capaldi appeared in.

It is nice in this special to see Bradley Walsh back as Graham. We missed Graham and it feels right to have him back for the end of Thirteen's adventures. It's a slight shame though that we don't see Ryan (presumably Tosin Cole was unavailable) one last time. Dan bows out of this episode early but he does return at the end. It's actually lovely to see Graham and Dan together at the end. These people are now bonded by their time with the Doctor. Best of all though is that we get to see David Bradley, Colin Baker, Peter Davison, Paul McGann, and Sylvester McCoy as their respective versions of the Doctor. This is a gimmick but a great gimmick all the same. It is strange really that they don't do this sort of thing more often in Doctor Who.

When we later got the 60th anniversary specials with Russell T Davies they were largely enjoyable (if not perfect) but the one disappointing thing is that they didn't really feel like anniversary specials or celebrations of Who. They just felt like some extra bonus episodes with Tennant and Catherine Tate. The Power of the Doctor on the other hand feels more like a true special in the way that it celebrates Doctor Who both past and present. The most memorable scenes come when Ace and Tegan meet their respective Doctors (or holographic versions of them anyway) again. Sylvester McCoy in particular is great in his scene with Sophie Aldred. The sequence where Jodie meets these morphing versions of her former self is also wonderfully done. When you watch this episode you can't help wondering how the Chibnall led team running Doctor Who can do great episodes like this and yet also turn out rubbish like Orphan 55 and Arachnids in the Uk. The gargantuan dips in quality during this era are quite baffling at times.

You could argue that The Power of the Doctor is an episode of great moments rather than a great episode but it works like gangbusters at its best. We have a good time, the cameos are fun, and it wraps up the end of Thirteen and regeneration in a satisfying way. One thing I like about this episode too is that it eschews the melodramatic and downbeat nature of the last two or three regenerations and has Thirteen embracing her fate in an accepting, even cheerful sort of way. This feels very in tone for Jodie's lighter and less abrasive version of the Doctor. If they had tried to make Jodie's regeneration all dark and maudlin and dragged it out I think it might have felt hollow and out of place. Chibnall, to his credit, also realises that less is sometimes more when it comes to regeneration scenes. "Tag, you're it!" is a much better sign off than the long rambling speech Peter Capaldi did before he regenerated.

Another thing I like about this episode too is that the Doctor, just for a change, regenerates on a cliff by the sea rather than inside an exploding TARDIS. It's something different and makes for a lovely shot with Segun Akinola's epic music. Another nice idea is the 'companions support group' at the end where we see some old faces and friends - most poignantly William Russell as Ian Chesterton. The Power of the Doctor is a very fanservice episode of Doctor Who but that's fine by me because I loved the cameos. All the fanservice works as a magical masking tape which disguises the traditional wonkiness of the story and parts of the production but, generally, I doff my cap to Chris Chibnall here because The Power of the Doctor is very enjoyable and serves as a nice last hurrah for Jodie.

Chris Chibnall's version of Doctor Who has been full of highs and lows (mostly lows if truth be told) and lots of middling episodes which were so boring you've forgotten them by the time the credits roll but at least he managed to end on a high. In a sense though episodes like this are doubly frustrating because they show that Chibnall was capable of doing really good stuff. The problem is he just didn't do it often enough. Although this episode is 87 minutes long it doesn't drag at all and I also like the fairly economical way it says farewell to

Jodie's Doctor at the end. We don't get drowned in melodrama or a long farewell tour. We simply get the Doctor saying goodbye to Yaz with ice cream and then embracing the regeneration in a dignified and refreshingly positive way.

Power of the Doctor is not perfect (I don't care too much for the wonky CGI train sequence at the start) but it is a lot of fun and all the callbacks and references to Doctors past makes it a treat for fans of Classic Who. The Power of the Doctor is both a celebration of Doctor Who and a memorable last hurrah for Jodie Whittaker. It is a pleasant surprise that this episode was so good after the disappointment of Legend of the Sea Devils. Jodie, as I've noted more than once in this book, is not my favourite Doctor and was sometimes quite hopeless in the part (not aided of course by some of the dreadful scripts) but she's good in this final special and despite all my complaints about this Doctor and this era I did feel a sense of loss as her time drew to a close at the end of this episode. If nothing else, Jodie's version of the Doctor was cheerful and friendly and maybe, in this grim and cynical age, that wasn't such a bad thing.

POSTSCRIPT

It is probably fair to say the Chris Chibnall era of Doctor Who was not looked upon as a golden era for the show. Of course, there were fans who liked this era and rated Jodie much more favourably than I did and that's fine because we all have our different opinions on things. I think that Peter Capaldi was probably the best Doctor since the show came back but others found Capaldi a bit cold and mannered. We all have different views. Some people love Matt Smith's Doctor while others found Matt Smith's Doctor a bit annoying.

I didn't find Jodie's Doctor very charismatic or interesting but there are of course fans who loved Jodie's Doctor. You can go on and on with all the Doctors. We all have our favourites and then others we didn't enjoy quite so much.

It wouldn't be unreasonable to say that the Chibnall era was far too often middling at best and dreadful at worst. The companions were a big problem in Chibnall's Who. There are too many of them. They don't get sufficient time on screen to register and are poorly written. Take Ryan for example. We know that his dad left and that in the first episode his grandmother died. Apart from that he is a complete blank. Chibnall gives Ryan some soap operish trappings, a vague sort of backstory, but Ryan does absolutely nothing. He doesn't develop as as a character, he is given nothing interesting to say or do. Yaz is even worse. Yaz is literally given nothing to do as a character. If Yaz had been played in series eleven by a stuffed toy it would have made no difference.

Graham, like Ryan, is given some (rather downbeat) soap operish back story and then given little to do. Graham is the only companion that registers though thanks entirely to Bradley Walsh. Walsh is a likeable and amusing screen presence. If anyone else had played Graham he probably would have been as boring as the others. Having all of these companions also diminishes Jodie's Doctor even further. She feels more like a supporting character than the Doctor. Chibnall's mistake is giving these characters a grounded sort of backstory but then not do anything with them in the actual show we are watching. By way of contrast, most of the companions in the Davies and Moffat era had an arc. They had a personality too.

Another problem with series eleven is the lack of an overall story arc. The stories in series eleven are not connected and exist in isolation. The only connective tissue that stands out is the return of the forgettable Stenza villain Tim Shaw in the finale. By this stage though we have completely forgotten about Tim Shaw and it feels like a huge anti-climax to bring him back. Russell T Davies gave you a Dalek fleet at the end of his first season. Steven Moffat brought back John Simm's Master at the end of Capaldi's last season. They were always building their seasons towards a big finale.

Remember how 'Bad Wolf' was a recurring symbol in the first season by Davies? We were intrigued to know where this was going. By contrast, Chibnall does absolutely nothing in series eleven to keep you interested. There is no arc or story thread that carries through the season. When Tim Shaw returns all you can hear is a collective sigh from the audience. That's it? Tim Shaw? That's the best you can do for a finale? Bring back a rubbish villain that we'd already forgotten? The show did improve after this but Chibnall had already done a lot of damage by now. I'd imagine there were a fair few fans who bailed out during series eleven through sheer boredom more than anything.

Chibnall's version of Doctor Who often felt dumbed down and yet it takes itself quite seriously. There is too much expositional dialogue. Everything is explained to you constantly and yet the actual stories (that are constantly being explained to us by the Doctor!) are often middling sort of affairs where nothing much happens. You know how with Davies and Moffat you had to sit through some 'filler' episodes to get to the good stuff? Those episodes where they are clearly treading water and saving the budget for something else? Examples of 'filler' episodes in Capaldi's last season would be things like Knock Knock and The Eaters of Light. These episodes, though not bad, seem sort of cheap and are a trifle on the dull side.

It doesn't matter though because you also get things like Oxygen and Thin Ice in that season. You'll also get the wonderful big two part finale of World Enough and Time and The Doctor Falls. You are rewarded for sitting through a few slightly forgettable episodes with plenty of good stuff elsewhere. Well, Chibnall's Doctor Who doesn't do this in series eleven. There is no reward for our time and patience. None at all. Series eleven is literally an entire season of dull 'filler' episodes of Doctor Who. Imagine if series ten had consisted entirely of episodes on a par with Eaters of the Light. It would have been slated wouldn't it? It would have been branded dull and lacking excitement. Series eleven is this doomsday scenario come to life.

Series eleven aired in the Autumn of 2018. The Woman Who Fell to Earth is the first episode and it's sort of alright. It's not bad. A bit dour maybe but not bad. You wouldn't say it was as good as The Eleventh Hour or Deep Breath but it's a mildly promising start to series eleven. Then we get The Ghost Monument - which is unbelievably boring. Then we get Rosa - which is a rather dull piece of drama featuring a sci-fi villain who may be the worst character in the history of Doctor Who. Then we get Arachnids in the UK - which is simply one of the worst episodes of Doctor Who ever made. Then we get The Tsuranga Conundrum - which arguably IS the worst episode of Doctor Who ever made. And so it goes on.

We soon had to accept a very painful truth in series eleven. Chibnall's Doctor Who is not very good. It's actually terrible. It is completely lifeless and flat. It doesn't engage. The stories are dull and feel like the first drafts of unfinished scripts that were rushed into production. The acting is wooden and you don't really care about any of these characters - including the

Doctor. You've seen better direction on CBBC shows than you get in series eleven. The new TARDIS interior is a cheap looking fiasco of design. They have crystal pillars that are clearly made out of plastic. The TARDIS interior is so small and cramped that they hardly have any TARDIS scenes in series eleven because it's almost impossible to film actors in there.

What made Chibnall most attractive to the BBC was his work as the creator and lead writer on the ITV drama Broadchurch. Chibnall was seen as a safe pair of hands. He was an experienced television writer and showrunner. Plus, he was a lifelong Doctor Who fan. What could possibly go wrong? The doubts - as far as Doctor Who fans were concerned - came from the episodes of Doctor Who that Chibnall had written. 42, The Hungry Earth/Cold Blood, Dinosaurs on a Spaceship, The Power of Three. None of these episodes were especially memorable. You wouldn't say any of them were very good.

Steven Moffat was always the obvious choice to replace Russell T Davies because he was clearly the stand-out guest writer during the Davies era. During the time that Davies was in charge of Doctor Who, Moffat wrote episodes like The Girl in the Fireplace, Blink, Silence in the Library, and The Empty Child. It was obvious that Moffat was the most talented contributor and the best person to be the new lead writer. With Chibnall it was far less clear cut. His contributions to Doctor Who as a guest writer had been average at best. They continued to be average in series eleven.

I wanted to love series eleven and I wanted to love Jodie. It gives me no pleasure to say that in series eleven Jodie Whittaker is absolutely terrible as the Doctor. We can't pretend that this is a memorable Doctor. This is the worst Doctor in the history of the show. Jodie seems to have based her entire performance on watching ten minutes of David Tennant in the part. There is no depth to her character. Jodie's Doctor essentially remains in limbo for the entire season with no development.

She gives her lines (and the mostly dreadful scripts are obviously no fault of poor Jodie) no weight or meaning or subtext. Jodie face scrunches and gurns her way through these episodes as if acting 'wacky' a character makes. She brings absolutely nothing to this part. Her Doctor has no sense of intrigue or danger. Her Doctor does not feel like a centuries old alien Time Lord. Jodie's Doctor feels like a patronising primary school teacher. This Doctor is so bland and uncharismatic that you almost forget she's supposed to be the Doctor at times.

Jodie's Doctor has no presence or gravitas and just fades into the background when the Doctor is supposed to be someone who can take charge of a situation through charismatic authority. And yet, because this was the first woman to play the Doctor, Jodie was mostly immune from criticism. Chibnall's masterstroke in a sense was that casting a woman as the Doctor made it less likely for people to point out how rubbish his version of Doctor Who was.

Segun Akinola, who replaced Gold, supplies an interesting score for Chibnall's Who. It's certainly not bad. But it isn't memorable in the way that Gold's music was and so the 'big' moments (not that there are any big moments in series eleven) don't get that grand sonic backdrop to amp them up and stir the emotions. Gold's themes for Matt Smith or Peter Capaldi were instantly recognisable. His themes for the companions were instantly recognisable - let alone his fantastic music for the Doctors. Akinola doesn't do anything like this for Who so his score just sort of becomes background noise. His music was ok, I quite liked it at times, but I'd struggle to remember any of it. When Murray Gold was the composer, you knew all the themes by heart.

So, series eleven has this firestorm of decisions which all proved to be miscalculations. The casting for Chibnall's Who wasn't very good. The choice of guest writers wasn't very good. The choice of directors clearly wasn't good (look at how flat and dull these episodes seem on the screen). The decision to make a season composed of self contained stories with no arc was obviously a mistake too. What is series eleven building towards? Absolutely nothing. After we've got the first episode (which introduces the new Doctor and companions) out of the way and then had the return of the TARDIS in episode two, you could show these episodes in any order you wanted to and it wouldn't make much difference. There is no sense of development or progress in series eleven.

The Doctor doesn't change at all. She feels no different in episode ten than she did in episode two. The companions don't change either. Ryan and Yaz in particular are as vague at the end of the series as they are at the start. There is no sense in series eleven that the showrunner has a vision for this show. There is no big idea or exciting plot arc. The characters are underwritten and the Doctor is too. It seems as if Chibnall wanted to make Doctor Who a bit simpler and less complex. There was nothing wrong with that. Most people probably thought Steven Moffat's Doctor Who got a bit too twisty and complicated at times. Chibnall however doesn't compensate for the elements he has removed.

The worst thing of all about series eleven is that it feels like it was conceived by someone who has no enthusiasm for this task. Just think of all the things you could potentially do if you were in charge of Doctor Who. Here's what Chibnall did in series eleven once he was in charge. (1) The Doctor lands in Sheffield where an alien with teeth in his face unwittingly kills an old lady when she falls off a crane. (2) The Doctor and her companions walk the length of a desert planet talking a lot. (3) The Doctor and her companions must alter bus timetables to stop a time travelling racist. (4) The Doctor and her companions wander around an empty hotel with a Donald Trumpish businessman.

(5) The Doctor wanders up and down the corridor of a spaceship talking to herself. (6) The gang experience the partition of India via a shed in the middle of nowhere. (7) The Doctor and her companions work in a warehouse. (8) The

Doctor and her companions are in 17th century England. They walk around a field a lot. Graham gets a funny hat to wear. (9) The Doctor and her companions land in Norway. A mirror is an alternate dimension where an entity takes on the form of a frog. (10) The villain with teeth in his face returns. The Doctor and her companions walk a lot.

Ok, so some of the sci-fi elements (giant spiders etc) are absent from these capsule summaries for comic effect but do you get the point? This is basically what series eleven offers. The only one of those that sounds interesting as an idea is number 9 - the synopsis for It Takes You Away. That's the only episode where someone has at least come up with an idea crazy enough to sound like a Doctor Who script. The rest of the writers in series eleven (of which Chibnall is far and away the biggest culprit) feel like they have gone out of their way to make the show boring.

Chibnall's tin ear for sci-fi and insistence on shoehorning dreary drama elements (the endless boring conversation Ryan has with his dad in Resolution in the cafe has already gone down in history as one of the dullest and most out of place moments in any Doctor Who episode) into his stories are like an anchor around the neck of series eleven. Chibnall's leisurely paced 'simpler' version of Doctor Who in series eleven is one of the most boring television shows I have ever watched in my entire life.

One of the worst things about Chibnall's Doctor Who is how it often feels like some middling American sci-fi show from the 1990s. It feels hopelessly dated and generic. You get the impression from Chibnall's Who that he is more of an RTD man than a Moffat fan. Chibnall feels like he has more in common with RTD than Moffat in the way that he gives Doctor Who more of a working-class domestic backdrop. The difference is that RTD can be funny. He could sprinkle his scripts with wit. RTD could also be completely crazy and give you really over the finales and big story arcs. Chibnall mimics the domestic backdrop of the RTD blueprint in series eleven but he doesn't bring the humour and fun to Doctor Who that RTD did.

Another weakness of Chibnall is, as we have mentioned, casting. Moffat cast Matt Smith and Peter Capaldi as the Doctor. He cast Michelle Gomez, Karen Gillan, Jenna Coleman, Pearl Mackie, and Arthur Darvill. RTD cast Christopher Eccleston and David Tennant as the Doctor. He also cast Billie Piper, Catherine Tate, John Barrowman, and John Simm. Chibnall cast Jodie Whittaker as the Doctor. He cast Tosin Cole and Mandip Gill. Chibnall basically cast the weakest ensemble of main actors the show has arguably ever endured.

Moffat and RTD clearly had a better nose for casting than Chibnall. They were able to get great actors for the lead regular roles on the show. And these actors were so good they could mitigate a terrible script. If an episode of Doctor wasn't brilliant in the Moffat or RTD era (and, let's be honest, not all of the episodes were brilliant) then you had a strong lead like Peter Capaldi who could still make the best of it. You would have Michelle Gomez lighting up the screen with dark comic charisma. You had lead actors like David Tennant and Matt Smith who were both charismatic enough to keep you engaged in a middling episode. You had Jenna Colman acting her socks off. You had John Barrowman having fun as Captain Jack. And so on.

In series eleven you have an ensemble who aren't capable of rising above this awful material. They sink with it. Bradley Walsh is one of the few good things about series eleven but he can't carry this show on his own. The Doctor should be the star. Bradley is doing what he's supposed to do. Supply an amusing supporting character. He has absolutely nothing to play off though. He might as well be standing in an empty TARDIS. Chibnall's version of Doctor Who in series eleven feels unfinished and rushed. It feels bland and unambitious. It feels like it is going through the motions and doing the bare minimum. It feels like a show made by people who can't be bothered. It feels like a show made by a showrunner who has no interest in science fiction and would be more at home writing on Holby City or Emmerdale.

Now, I'm sure the people who worked on series eleven were doing their best. They didn't set out to make a boring show. The fault then lies with Chibnall. He is the showrunner. He is to blame for the dull scripts and lack of ambition. It was Chibnall who wrote several (mostly terrible scripts) for series eleven and then recruited a bunch of writers with no background in fantasy or science fiction. It was Chibnall who decided that series eleven would have no arc or ongoing story. It was Chibnall who chose the directors.

There are lifelong Doctor Who fans who bailed out during season eleven let alone casual viewers! I do not blame anyone who lost interest in Doctor Who during series eleven. Like many Doctor Who fans, I was dismayed and shocked at how bad series eleven was when it finally hit the screen. Moffat and Davies might have stretched our patience at times and dropped the odd duff episode but they never served up constant unrelenting mediocrity in the way that series eleven did. Even their worst scripts were festooned with more wit, imagination, and subtlety than anything to drop from the pen of Chris Chibnall in series eleven.

Anyway, what about series twelve? Was it better? Had Chris Chibnall learned any lessons? Well, yes and no, but mostly yes. What about the clunky social messages of Chris Chibnall's Who? Has the obvious politics been toned down in series twelve? To a degree although it is surely not a coincidence that the three episodes in series twelve that are preaching to us in the most obvious way (Orphan 55, Praxeus, and Can You Hear Me?) have the lowest audience ratings when it comes to AI.

Chris Chibnall apparently hasn't quite deduced yet in series twelve that people do not tune into Doctor Who to get a patronising lecture about microplastics or the importance of mental health. They already know about these things themselves thank you very much. Put the message in the subtext of a good science fiction story. There it will resonate. Do not broadcast the message with a loudspeaker in a story that is bland and forgettable. People will take more notice of a message in something they liked. If they get a clunky message in something they didn't like they are simply going to be annoyed and feel like they are being patronised by people who have made them sit through something awful.

What about the cast in series twelve? Are they any better? It's somewhat more difficult to be positive in this area. Jodie Whittaker does seem to improve in the Spyfall openers. For the first time we see her Doctor angry, morose, sad, and distant. We see, for the first time, a real sense of an inner life. But then for large tracts of series twelve the Doctor is back to her usual bouncy, lightweight, and, well, annoying self. You always get a sense that Jodie could have made a better fist of this character with better writing but was rather hamstrung by Chris Chibnall. Chibnall, for reasons best known to himself, made the first female Doctor weak and lightweight.

When one looks at Doctor Who post 2005 you can't imagine anyone else who would have been as popular as David Tennant. That was clearly genius casting. You can't imagine anyone who would have been as good as Peter Capaldi was in the part. Capaldi might not have been a hit with casual audiences in the way that Tennant was but it was great casting all the same. Matt Smith and Christopher Eccleston were probably not quite everyone's cup of tea (I'd probably include myself in this as I found Matt Smith a bit grating in the end) but they were strong lead actors for the show.

Smith dominated the screen with his energy and eccentricity and Eccleston was brilliant in dramatic scenes. Jodie Whittaker, in comparison, feels like the first time the part has been miscast since the show returned. Jodie doesn't really bring anything of her own to the part (unless of course you count appearing to be out of breath all the time as she grapples with dialogue). You can't help thinking that there are many actors, of any gender, who would have made a better Doctor than Jodie.

As for the 'fam', Ryan and Yaz still fail to make much of an impression in series twelve. These are surely two of the most forgettable companions in the long history of Doctor Who. Bradley Walsh is still enjoyable as Graham though. Series twelve showed signs of improvement but, ultimately, you still remained unconvinced that Chibnall and Jodie were the best custodians that Doctor Who could have chosen to replace Moffat and Capaldi. All the optimism that heralded the arrival of The Woman Who Fell to Earth seemed like a very long time ago now.

The viewing figures that greeted the start of series eleven seem like the top of Mount Everest after the alarming drop in ratings for series twelve. And yet, series twelve was better and the viewing figures still dropped. It wasn't a classic season but it had some good episodes. It wasn't boring in the way that series eleven was. You could argue that some of the story decisions Chris Chibnall made were baffling but he managed to deliver a better season of television. The audience though seem to have lost interest.

The large audiences that Doctor Who used to attract in the David Tennant era feel like a very distant memory indeed. The frustrating thing is that the audience is still out there somewhere. Ten million people watched The Woman Who Fell to Earth. Naturally, it would have been difficult to maintain those figures because many tuned in out of curiosity to watch the first female Doctor. Difficult but not impossible. We've seen shows like The Bodyguard attract and keep huge audiences.

In series eleven, apart from The Woman Who Fell to Earth, I didn't like a single episode. In series twelve though I Liked both Spyfall episodes, The Haunting of Villa Diodati, Fugitive of the Judoon, and Ascension of the Cybermen. I also thought Nikola Tesla's Night of Terror was passable and although I didn't care too much for the Timeless Children I didn't think it was terrible in the way that some of the series eleven episodes were. So, for me, the show improved a lot in series twelve. It was much more watchable. There was an arc, bigger stakes, more to react to. Chibnall got better at doing Doctor Who.

This was evident too in Flux which, while far from perfect, was something that I generally enjoyed. In a sense then Chris Chibnall proved people like me wrong in the end because we'd written him off entirely after series eleven but he managed to up his game and do some decent stuff. I think Flux is the sort of thing that Chibnall should have done from the start rather than the tedious series eleven episodes. Chibnall was clearly more at home writing one big ongoing story than he was having to come up with a new fresh idea each week. I even enjoyed John Bishop as Dan in Flux and beyond so I give Chris Chibnall credit for that casting. Flux is not brilliant. It isn't amazing. But it is pretty entertaining and in the Chibnall era we'll take whatever we can get.

As for the specials, the first two Dalek ones were middling and forgettable. Eve of the Daleks was quite nifty though if not something that would win Doctor Who any new converts. Then we had Legend of the Sea Devils and The Power of the Doctor. One of the worst episodes of Doctor Who ever made followed by one of the most memorable NuWho episodes. Talk about the ridiculous and the sublime. This was Chris Chibnall in a nutshell. Embarrassingly bad one episode and surprisingly good the next. His era was truly all over the place at times.

The era of Chris Chibnall was not a great success. It often felt like we something we had to endure rather than something we enjoyed or looked forward to. Series eleven was truly a disaster but it did get better. It didn't get better often enough to put Chibnall on the level of Moffat or Davies but it could have been worse. Chibnall did at least manage to salvage some dignity before his tenure ended.

I don't think the Chris Chibnall era will ever be looked back upon as some lost gem that was unfairly overlooked at the time. It is possible though that we might look back on it with more fondness one day purely for the fact that it was its own thing with its new cameras, crowded TARDIS, and lack of Murray Gold. And maybe Chibnall's Who was more influential than we give it credit for. The Toymaker dancing to The Spice Girls in The Giggle? Well, that was surely inspired by the Master and the Rasputin song in The Power of the Doctor wasn't it?

MY TOP TEN BEST EPISODES OF THE CHIBNALL/JODIE ERA

(1) SPYFALL PART 1
(2) THE POWER OF THE DOCTOR
(3) VILLAGE OF THE ANGELS
(4) THE HAUNTING OF VILLA DIODATI
(5) SPYFALL PART 2
(6) THE WOMAN WHO FELL TO EARTH
(7) FUGITIVE OF THE JUDOON
(8) ASCENSION OF THE CYBERMEN
(9) WAR OF THE SONTARANS
(10) EVE OF THE DALEKS

MY TOP TEN WORST EPISODES OF THE CHIBNALL/JODIE ERA

(1) ORPHAN 55
(2) THE TSURANGA CONUNDRUM
(3) ARACHNIDS IN THE UK
(4) LEGEND OF THE SEA DEVILS
(5) PRAXEUS
(6) THE BATTLE OF RANSKOOR AV KOLOS
(7) KERBLAM!
(8) ROSA
(9) DEMONS OF THE PUNJAB
(10) CAN YOU HEAR ME?

Photo Credit

https://unsplash.com/photos/a-video-game-with-a-spaceship-and-stars-in-the-sky-lXf1xS1bR2A

Gregory Stewart

2022